THE ART OF WAR
FOR WRITERS

fiction writing strategies, tactics, and exercises

JAMES SCOTT BELL

WRITER'S DIGEST BOOKS
Cincinnati, Ohio
www.writersdigest.com

For more resources for writers, visit www.writersdigest.com/books.

To receive a free weekly e-mail newsletter delivering tips and updates about writing and about Writer's Digest products, register directly at http://newsletters. fwpublications.com.

13 12 11 10   5 4 3 2

Distributed in Canada by Fraser Direct
100 Armstrong Avenue
Georgetown, Ontario, Canada L7G 5S4
Tel: (905) 877-4411

Distributed in the U.K. and Europe by David & Charles
Brunel House, Newton Abbot, Devon, TQ12 4PU, England
Tel: (+44) 1626-323200, Fax: (+44) 1626-323319
E-mail: postmaster@davidandcharles.co.uk

Distributed in Australia by Capricorn Link
P.O. Box 704, Windsor, NSW 2756 Australia
Tel: (02) 4577-3555

Library of Congress Cataloging-in-Publication Data
Bell, James Scott.
  The art of war for writers : fiction writing strategies, tactics, and exercises /
James Scott Bell.
    p. cm.
  Includes index.
  ISBN 978-1-58297-590-0 (pbk. : alk. paper)
  1. Fiction--Technique. 2. Fiction--Authorship. I. Title.
  PN3355.B36 2009
  808.3--dc22   2009032799

Edited by Kelly Nickell
Interior designed by Terri Woesner
Cover designed by Grace Ring
Production coordinated by Mark Griffin

Dedication

This book is dedicated to my motivation, inspiration,
great love, and first editorial eye—my wife, Cindy.

TABLE *of* CONTENTS

PART III: STRATEGY 184

Introduction

Sun Tzu, so far as we know, never wrote a novel.

Nor did he live in L.A., which makes it nearly certain he never tried his hand at a screenplay.

What we do know is that the author of *The Art of War* was a Chinese general writing sometime between 400–320 B.C. who recorded his aphorisms based upon actual experience in the field.

The approach to war in Sun Tzu's day was a chaotic mess. By bringing orderly principles to bear, he enabled generals to finally achieve clarity in planning for battle.

The publishing business is a messy affair, too. There are many obstacles on the way to publication—including one's own mental state—that it seems daunting and downright hostile out there.

What I want to do with this collection is offer you some helpful observations based on more than twenty years in the fiction writing game. This is *not* a comprehensive "how to" on fiction. I've written two other books in that form. Rather, I seek to fill in some "cracks" in what is normally taught in writing books and classes.

I still read books on writing. My philosophy is if I find just one thing of value, even if it's only a new take on something I already know, it's worth it. Anything that helps me become a better writer, I want to find. That's the spirit I hope permeates this text.

Because I am, like you, a writer. We understand each other. We are not like other people. We are, in fact, pitiable wretches.

Let me explain.

Back in the 1940s, a novelist named Jack Woodford gave advice to young writers, among which was the following:

> So there you are. A free-lance writer! Oh pitiable wretch! Oh miserable fool! Of all the business you could have gone into—operating a movie theatre, or making guns, running a drug store or learning how to be a tailor or a plumber, a typographer or a hot dog cook—you insist on going into the business of cash and carry prose. Well, you know best. As for me, I know there isn't a so-and-so thing I can do to discourage you or make you change your mind. I admit (reluctantly) I've made a pretty good thing out of it myself. *But* I've had some breaks ... Can *you* be sure of getting breaks? Of course you can't. That's what a break means—a stroke of luck that nobody expects, all pine for madly, and mighty few ever get. Where

would I have been without my breaks? God knows. I don't!

—Jack Woodford, *How to Write for Money*

So *The Art of War for Writers* is my modest attempt at a field manual for all writing wretches, because I know how hard it is out there. Following Sun Tzu's example, I'll keep the subjects compact, subsumed under three main areas:

1. **RECONNAISSANCE.** This section is primarily about the mental game of writing, because what happens in your head affects everything else.

Dick Simon, of Simon & Schuster fame, once said, "All writers without exception are scared to death. Some simply hide it better than others." Mental landmines are everywhere and, if not cleared, will keep you from producing words that sell.

A successful writing career must be built upon mental discipline. That doesn't mean you have to give up your role as the town eccentric. It does mean you have to write smart if you want to get published.

2. **TACTICS.** Here, we'll talk about craft. I've taught writing for fifteen years and written a couple of books and numerous articles on it. I've also benefited from writing books and articles myself, none of which I throw away, and all of which make my living space smaller.

战 3 争

What I want to provide in this section are practical tactics and techniques to help you go *deeper*, to do things that will set you apart from all the vanilla slush that's poured into the offices of tired editors and agents.

Think of these as the extras Q gives James Bond. You know, like cufflinks that are really flame throwers. Pens that turn into parachutes. That sort of thing. (See also "Utilize the Q Factor as a strategic weapon for motivation at just the right time." on page 136.)

These are all techniques to put in your toolbox, ready to use on your novel.

I've seen a great many manuscripts in the last few years that have been very good, yet failed to sell. The writing was solid, the characters and plot workmanlike, the structure sound.

Yet, no placement. Why not? Because *good enough* isn't good enough anymore.

Sun Tzu understood that it was the accumulation of small advantages that added up to long-term victory. You need to view your manuscripts the same way.

And here's the good news. If you can take just one aspect of your writing to that storied "next level," it will be quite evident to an agent or editor. They see so much that is mediocre that their literary eyes will light up with delight at seeing something better.

3. **STRATEGY.** Finally, I offer some advice on the no man's land of the publishing biz. Anything can happen here,

战 4 争

and often does. You have to be aware of the possibilities, and take a long, strategic view of your career.

Simply put, you must be devoted to quality.

It's no secret what happened to the Detroit automakers in the 1970s and '80s. They put out products inferior to the Japanese who were excelling in both design and reliability. As a result, Detroit car manufacturers dug themselves into a hole from which they have never fully recovered.

In any enterprise, quality is job one. Quality is defined by two things:

1. appeal of the workmanship
2. absence of defects

Never flag in the pursuit of writing excellence, for that is your workmanship. The Japanese were inspired by the concept of *kaizen*, the philosophy of seeking constant improvement in all aspects of business, every day, all the time.

At the same time, keep learning about the common defects found in unsuccessful writing and in the operations of the publishing world—so you won't engage in them.

Sun Tzu wrote: "He wins his battles by making no mistakes."

My hope is that this manual will help you avoid mistakes and write stronger books and win the battle to get and stay published.

part 1

RECONNAISSANCE

Thus, what enables the wise sovereign and the good general to strike and conquer, and achieve things beyond the reach of ordinary men, is foreknowledge.

—Sun Tzu

Baseball is 90 percent mental—the other half is physical.

—Yogi Berra

The writer who observes the battlefield before entering the fray will be better equipped to plan strategy and tactics.

War, according to Sun Tzu, is about adaptability and the taking advantage of opportunities.

That's where reconnaissance comes in. Reconnaissance is the gathering of information, based on observations behind enemy lines, for military purposes.

Reconnaissance lets you know what you're up against.

It enables you to work smart.

To begin our own reconnoitering, let's get an aerial view of the publishing business. What do we see down there?

A great big dollar sign, that's what we see.

Write this down: It's about money.

The publishing business *is* a business, and businesses need to make a profit.

"Wait," comes the protest. "You mean to tell me it's not about passion for great writing? Not about agents and editors and publishers who truly care about good books?"

Yes, these people do exist. Without them, publishing would have no heart. But they are constrained in their efforts by that ubiquitous arbiter of all things corporate and commercial, the bottom line. If they can merge art and commerce, happy day! But commerce eventually controls.

Do you seek a career as a novelist? Then you need to know that it comes down to a simple query: Will you be of value to a publisher?

The publishing business has always been undergirded by monetary calculation. Even when Maxwell Perkins was snifting brandy and wading through a trunk of Thomas Wolfe pages. Even when Bennett Cerf was plucking his tie nervously because Ayn Rand refused to allow *Atlas Shrugged* to be cut.

Yes, even when Fitzgerald was boozing and Hemingway was running from the bulls, it's always been about the money because no business can continue to run unless it turns a profit.

If anything has changed, it's that this calculus has picked up speed. In the "old days," a publishing house might have carried promising talent along for a number of books, hoping they'd catch on.

Not so today. Corporate consolidations demand quarterly profits, so money has to be made, and fast.

As the legendary ad man David Ogilvy once put it, "In the modern world of business, it is useless to be a creative original unless you can also sell what you create."

So, as one who wants to make a career out of fiction writing, you simply must show the publisher your value, now and in the future.

战 **9** 争

Publishers are not interested in publishing a novel. They want to publish *novelists*, writers who can build readerships and make money for the company over the long term. You need to position yourself as someone who can deliver the goods.

Does this mean not writing what you love?

No. But write what you love with eyes wide open.

02

The writer must understand the essentials of success for a long-term writing career, and count the cost accordingly.

Assuming you have decided to forge ahead toward a fiction-writing career, let me give you the ten characteristics you must possess (or develop).

1. **DESIRE.** It's got to be a hunger inside you. You're going to have to sacrifice time and money and endure frustrations galore. If you don't have the desire, you won't last long out there on the battlefield.

2. **DISCIPLINE.** It's all about production. A quota of words, six days a week.

3. **COMMITMENT TO CRAFT.** You can't just dash off a book. Leonard Bishop wrote, "Dramatic characters, inventive plotlines, exciting and intense situations are not achieved through accident or 'good luck.' The writers of great books zealously learn the craft of their profession so they can release the power and depth of their imagination and experience."

4. **PATIENCE.** It takes time. But you can cut down the time if you have 1, 2, and 3.

5. **HONESTY.** Be willing to confront your weaknesses as a writer.

6. **WILLINGNESS TO LEARN.** No chip on your shoulder. Check your ego at the door, or wherever else is convenient.

7. **BUSINESS-LIKE ATTITUDE.** Develop business savvy and professionalism.

8. **RHINO SKIN.** Learn from every rejection, and never let any rejection hold you back.

9. **LONG-TERM VIEW.** Don't think: "Do I have a book inside me?" Think: "Do I have a writer inside me?"

   And answer: "Yes!"

> If someone who writes that badly can become a writer, then even the dippiest of us can become a writer, chacma baboons can become writers, sludge and amoeba can become writers. The trick is not in *becoming* a writer, it is in *staying* a writer. Day after week after month after year. Staying in there for the long haul.
>
> —Harlan Ellison

10. **TALENT.** The least important. Everyone has some talent. It's what you do with it that counts.

How'd you do on that list? If you see any weaknesses, are you confident that you can turn them around?

You can, you know. Start by writing down your honest reactions to the following statements:

> I decided that I would continue to write as long as I lived, even if I never sold one thing, because that was what I wanted out of my life.
>
> —George Bernau

Your reaction

_____

_____

_____

_____

_____

_____

_____

_____

_____

_____

_____

_____

_____

You must want it *enough*. Enough to take all the rejections, enough to pay the price of disappointment and discouragement while you are learning. Like any other artist you must learn your craft—then you can add all the genius you like.

—Phyllis Whitney

Your reaction

_____

_____

_____

_____

_____

_____

_____

_____

_____

_____

_____

In Boot Camp, tough sergeants deliberately try to break the morale of inducted men. Those who break they send back to civilian life, or to some more or less ignominious chore in army life. There are two or three hundred thousand 'writers' who 'write at' writing in this country. Ninety percent of them make next to nothing. The few who do get

by are those who were not "broken" in the Boot
Camp of their own wills, or lack of same.

—Jack Woodford

Your reaction

_____

_____

_____

_____

_____

_____

_____

_____

_____

_____

A year from now, look at the quotes again, and write
new responses. What is the trajectory of your writing life?
How have you grown as a writer? What new things have
you learned about the profession and the craft?

Reflect. Review. Replan.

Be stern in the council-chamber, so that you may
control the situation.

—Sun Tzu

03

Know the difference
between a hero and a fool.

In battle, the generals don't want fools rushing in. A fool is not only likely to get shot, he can also bring the enemy storming down on his fellows.

A hero follows orders, but then performs "above and beyond the call of duty."

Yes, sometimes a fool can become a hero by accident. But most of the time the fool just ends up dead.

It's always better to know the difference, and aspire to the heroic.

If you want to be a writer, know this:

A hero knows it takes hard work and a long time to get published; a fool thinks it should happen immediately, because he thinks he's a hero already.

A hero learns the craft; a fool doesn't think there's much to learn.

A hero keeps growing all his writing life; a fool thinks he's fully grown already.

A hero fights to make his writing worthy, even when no one's noticing; a fool demands to be noticed all the time, even if his writing stinks.

A hero is persistent and professional; a fool is insistent and annoying.

A hero gets knocked down and quietly regroups to write again; a fool gets knocked down and whines about it ever after.

A hero makes his luck; a fool cries about how unlucky he is.

A hero recognizes the worth in others; a fool can't believe others are worth more than he.

A hero keeps writing, no matter what, knowing effort is its own reward; a fool eventually quits and complains that the world is unfair.

Be a hero.

A foundation in discipline is always the first step toward victory.

Victory in anything, from war to football, is founded in training and discipline. Nothing worthwhile is gained by sloth and wishful thinking.

It's not the will to win that counts, but the will *to prepare* to win.

That said, there is one discipline that stands above all else in the quest for writing success. I was fortunate to get this lesson early in my writing pursuit, and took it to heart. It is the single biggest reason I was published in the first place, and have produced the books I have.

It is, simply, this:

WRITE A QUOTA OF WORDS EVERY WEEK

Anthony Trollope was working for the British postal service and trying to become accepted as a novelist when he began a quota system for is writing. He wrote in his autobiography:

> There was no day on which it was my positive duty to write for the publishers, as it was my duty

> to write reports for the Post Office. I was free to be idle if I pleased. But as I had made up my mind to undertake this second profession, I found it to be expedient to bind myself by certain self-imposed laws. When I have commenced a new book, I have always prepared a diary, divided into weeks, and carried it on for the period which I have allowed myself for the completion of the work. In this I have entered, day by day, the number of pages I have written, so that if at any time I have slipped into idleness for a day or two, the record of that idleness has been there, staring me in the face and demanding of me increased labor, so that the deficiency might be supplied.

The daily recording of the number of words you write is an invaluable incentive to get your work done. But set your goals on a weekly basis, as Trollope did. "According to the circumstances of the time—whether my other business might be then heavy or light, or whether the book which I was writing was or was not wanted with speed—I have allotted myself so many pages a week."

If something comes up on one day that prevents you from writing your quota, you just make it up later in the week.

Do you think that such a mechanical recording system is beneath the inspired artist? Trollope was told the same thing.

战 **19** 争

I have been told that such appliances are beneath the notice of a man of genius. I have never fancied myself to be a man of genius, but had I been so I think I might well have subjected myself to these trammels. Nothing, surely, is so potent as a law that may not be disobeyed. It has the force of the water drop that hollows the stone. A small daily task, if it be really daily, will beat the labors of a spasmodic Hercules. ...

I have known authors whose lives have always been troublesome and painful because their tasks have never been done in time. ... Publishers have distrusted them, and they have failed to write their best because they have seldom written at ease. I have done double their work—though burdened with another profession—and have done it almost without an effort. ... And that little diary, with its dates and ruled spaces, its record that must be seen, its daily, weekly demand upon my industry, has done all that for me.

Trollope's parting advice still rings true today:

... I therefore venture to advise young men who look forward to authorship as the business of their lives, even when they propose that that authorship should be of the highest class known, to avoid enthusiastic rushes with their pens and to seat

themselves at their desks day by day, as though
they were lawyers' clerks; and so let them sit until
the allotted task shall be accomplished.

If you're going to be obsessive about anything in the
writing business, make it your word quota.

05

Career fiction writers must be aware of what the successful writing life is like.

A friend of mine, Terri Blackstock, a highly successful novelist, wrote the following about the writing life. It's worth your attention, especially if you think getting published means the end of all your worries. It is produced here with her permission:

⌣

I think one of the things unique to the writer's life is that we do seem to be on a roller coaster. I finish a book! Hoorah! Everything's wonderful.

Then I send it off and wait. Time passes. My spirits plunge. It's the worst thing I've ever written. Why, oh why did I send it when I did? I start scouring the newspaper for real jobs.

Then I get the call. They love it and are really going to publish it. Yes! Life is grand! Woo-hoo!

Then I get the revision letter. It's horrible. They want me to rewrite the whole book, change the title, and think about a pseudonym. They hate the plot and think the wrong characters died. Oh, and they want me to add a dog and a baby. I plunge again as I try to pick up the pieces that are salvageable.

But then it occurs to me how it can be done, and hey, that dog really does add to the suspense, and the baby will be worth a few boxes of tissue, so yahoo, I'm up again as I send it off. It's the best thing I've ever done, a guaranteed blockbuster.

But then I can't pay my light bill, and the checks are starting to bounce, and that check from the publisher never comes. So I plunge again. Finally, I get paid, and dance around singing "I'm in the money!" Then I write a check to Uncle Sam, pay that late light bill, pay my life insurance premium that I'm behind on, and wonder how I'm going to make it on what's left over until the next check. Spirits take another dive.

Book comes out, good review, I dance again and sing for joy and write all my friends and make copies for my mother. Then I go on Amazon and read one lousy review from some hostile reader, and I notice that I'm ranked 6,000,342,786, and I go around the house looking for my gun or the Valium I threw away when I was dancing for joy that last time.

But before I pull the trigger or toss those pills down my throat, I start thinking, "What if some guy had a gun and a bottle of anxiety pills and before he offs himself a shot rings out and he hits the floor and suddenly wants

战23争

to live, only others want him dead," and woo-hoo, my spirits soar and my eyes glaze over, and like a homing robot (if there's such a thing), I stumble back to that keyboard and start typing.

And it all starts over again.

That's the writing life.

06

A wise and well-respected writer once said, "Nobody knows anything." Listen to him.

William Goldman, legendary screenwriter of such classic films as *Butch Cassidy and the Sundance Kid* and *All the President's Men*, had an axiom about Hollywood: *Nobody knows anything.*

I have often said to writers that the publishing business should not even be called a "business" from our side of things. In business, you can do market research and anticipate a certain amount of return for a certain amount of effort.

Not so the writer. There's no guarantee of *any* return on our investment of time and effort.

And while for the publishers it is all about the bottom line, they aren't guaranteed a hit every time, either.

What makes a successful book or career is something of a mystery. Every now and then some new writer hits it big, and everybody tries to figure out why. But that's only after the fact. Trying to make it happen again almost never works.

Curtis Sittenfeld's novel *Prep* was published with a low advance and low expectations. Then the thing sold

133,000 copies in hardcover. The paperback did boffo, the movie rights were optioned.

So Ms. Sittenfeld got a new two-book deal with a huge advance and marketing effort. But her second novel, *The Man of My Dreams*, disappointed.

As Ms. Sittenfeld herself put it, "People think publishing is a business, but it's a casino."

Charles Frazier's *Cold Mountain* was a surprise sensation, selling 1.6 million copies in hardcover.

So ... he was given $8 million for his next one, *Thirteen Moons*. The publisher printed 750,000 copies. About 240,000 were sold. Leaving maybe $7 million of the advance unearned.

"It's guesswork," said Bill Thomas, editor in chief of Doubleday Broadway.

So, what can you do about the guesswork?

Your job.

Which is the page in front of you. Making it the best it can be.

More on how to do that in "Part II: Tactics."

Whining will not help you win the battle for publication.

Every moment spent whining about your writing career is a moment of creative energy lost.

Christina Katz, author of *Get Known Before the Book Deal*, suggests writers sign a statement that includes:

> I, _____, being of sound mind and body, do solemnly commit to keep my grousing to myself for the period of one year. This stuffing of a sock into my mouth includes, but is not limited to, whining about all matters related to the publication of my work. I will not grumble ... I will not cry ... I will not moan.

Turn grousing into energy, by writing.

08

"Do the thing you fear, and the death of fear is certain."[1]

The biggest mental obstacle—in writing, in war, in life itself—is fear.

Fear paralyzes. It shrinks the mental faculties. It keeps us from action, in this case, writing words in order to get them published.

And while fear is a fact of existence, it need not lead to defeat.

Consider a certain amount of fear to be a built-in mechanism to keep us alert. That's really what it is. It shows you are engaged and awake and not a lawn chair.

Now, the writing life is full of fears. Fear of not being good enough; of not getting published; of getting published and not selling; of getting published once and never again; of getting stomped by critics (even those within your own family). Fear that your mother will be disappointed in what you've written, or your father will think you're just wasting your life.

Dwell too much on these fears and you can become catatonic. I know of one writer who had an initial success and never wrote another thing for publication, so afraid

---

1 Ralph Waldo Emerson.

was he that he would be ripped by the critics. I even know another writer who is one of the most gifted stylists I've ever run across, but who has never submitted anything for publication for fear he'll be rejected.

Yes, fear is real, but so is the answer.

Young Teddy Roosevelt found it. He was a frail, sickly child, afraid of many things. So he stayed inside his house a lot and read books, mainly adventure stories. One day he was reading a novel by the English author Frederick Marryat. In his autobiography, Roosevelt records what happened:

> In this passage the captain of some small British man-of-war is explaining to the hero how to acquire the quality of fearlessness. He says that at the outset almost every man is frightened when he goes into action, but that the course to follow is for the man to keep such a grip on himself that he can act just as if he was not frightened. After this is kept up long enough it changes from pretense to reality, and the man does in very fact become fearless by sheer dint of practicing fearlessness when he does not feel it.

From that day on, TR determined to live his life just that way, and did indeed become a man known for his boldness and vigor.

As a writer, you can live the TR way:

1. Determine that you will *act* as if you had no fear. Act as if you *are* a successful writer. Don't do this with arrogance, but with determination.

2. Don't wait for your feelings to change; turn fear into energy for writing. When a wave of anxiety hits you, channel it in your writing. If you can go somewhere and write at that very moment, so much the better. Even if it's in a journal or on a napkin. Write.

3. Set writing goals that challenge you. Then take an immediate step toward that goal. (See "You are a business, and your books are the product." on page 186.)

09

The outsized ego is not a weapon of value.

You write because you believe you have something worth a reader's time. This is not necessarily an act of pure, unadulterated ego. It is an act of *confidence* based upon *mutual exchange*. You are offering something of value to a consumer.

But because it is such a personal act—it's all coming from one source, you—the ego can easily become inflated or deflated. In either case, you've got to be ready to put the ego where it belongs—out of the way.

Praise might be heaped on you, and that's not always a good thing. You can, as the saying goes, start believing your own press. You may be tempted to go on cruise control with your writing.

Or, worse, you may feel so much pressure to live up to the praise that you freeze up. One form of this is the infamous "second-book syndrome" that many "overnight successes" have suffered through.

On the other end of the scale, getting slammed by critics or readers can easily turn your ego into a Hindenburg.

You can start by expecting to be hammered by the small. Robert Crais, the great Los Angeles noir writer, noted once that "the world is full of haters," and he gets some of their e-mail. He has an assistant weed those out and doesn't even read them.

So don't let success make you or failure break you.

And don't confuse ego with self-confidence.

I've spoken to experienced writer friends about this. There seems to be a rise in the arrogant up-and-comer variety of unpubbed (or self-pubbed) writer. They are "know-it-alls" even though they have never had a book published, or have only forked out dough to have a vanity press bring out their book.

It's as if they think aggressive and uncivil egocentrism can hurtle them to the front of the author pack, where their narcissism demands they be ensconced. They think they can get there without doing the hard work of learning the craft and growing as a writer.

Listen, being a published writer is a privilege you earn. You're not going to earn it by tooting a horn no one wants to hear. You're going to earn it by knuckling down and writing, and letting the writing itself do the tooting for you.

When the day comes that your book does appear, you of course can undertake promotion and marketing. By then, it will make sense to let the world know your book is out.

Status, worry, and comparison are ways to madness, not victory.

One of the biggest obstacles of all comes from comparison with other writers and worrying about your status in the publishing world. This is the way to ultimate madness. The writing life is crazy enough without you making it worse on yourself.

> I don't feel in competition with other writers. Because I don't write about the same things as any other writer that I know of does.
>
> —Truman Capote

Best-selling novelist Tess Gerritsen has the following advice, which she graciously gave me permission to reproduce here:

STOP CHECKING YOUR AMAZON INDEX

Yep, that means you. Unless you're checking the effectiveness of a particular promotional tool (in which case you may want to see how the index responds), you really shouldn't be looking at yourself on Amazon at all. In particular, avoid looking at the reader reviews of your books. Some of those readers are nasty, vicious people, and why do you want to torture yourself by reading a lousy review of your latest book? Sure, you may find a really great review, and that'll make you feel good ... for about an hour. But a lousy review will leave you feeling miserable for a week. You wouldn't volunteer to get your fingernails wrenched off with pliers, would you? So why let anonymous readers torture you on Amazon?

STOP GOOGLING YOURSELF

For the same reason, I told you not to look up your own books on Amazon. Sure, maybe you'll find a website that says nice things about you. But you might also find a site that calls you the spawn of Satan. So don't even look. Because ignorance truly is bliss.

LEARN TO SAY NO

Writers are often told to jump at every chance to promote ourselves. So we accept every invitation to speak at libraries, schools and writers' conferences. We'll travel a thousand miles, take three days off from our writing, to smile at a gathering and sell only thirty books. When you're starting off and still trying to establish your name, these are probably good investments of your time. But you have to learn when enough is enough. Don't let the gigs take over your calendar. Don't let them eat too deeply into your writing time.

EXERCISE

Last autumn, I sprained my knee while hiking down a mountain. For two months, I could barely walk, much less hike. Stuck at home, I got grumpy and flabby. Then winter set in, and the roads got icy, prolonging my inactivity. Finally I got fed up with how listless I felt and made one of the best investments of my life: I bought a treadmill. It sits right here in my office, and it's my new best friend. First thing in the morning, I turn on NPR on the radio, climb onto the treadmill, and take a brisk uphill walk for half an hour. When I'm done, I feel pumped and ready to dive into my writing. And I can stop feeling guilty about my sedentary job.

> I think comparisons are odious.
>
> —John Madden

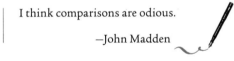

CHASE OTHER INTERESTS

Indulge your hobbies. Feed your curiosity. Life isn't just about meeting deadlines and seeing another one of your books on the stands; life is also about doing and learning cool stuff. We get about eight decades on this earth. That seems like a lot of time, but as I get older, I realize how precious little time that really is. Although I spend most of the year racing to meet my book deadlines, I'm also learning how to read ancient Greek. I'm trying to read through my copy of Herodotus, which sits on my nightstand. I'm trying to memorize a Chopin Ballade on the piano. Probably none of these hobbies will end up being used in a book, but why does everything have to be about the writing?

To keep from turning off those who can publish you, you must not be desperate.

An agent I know was once at a large writers' conference, hosting a table at dinner. The table was one of dozens, and each table was full. He was right in the middle of saying something to one of the conferees when he felt a tug on his sleeve. A woman was literally on her knees, saying, "I beg you to be my agent. I *beg* you to be my agent."

That's desperation.

He did not become her agent.

A well-known editor with a big publishing house reported the following: "During the cesarean section birth of my daughter twelve years ago, I sat perched on a stool, gloved and gowned, next to a chatty anesthesiologist. As the operation got underway she asked about my job. Once she heard, she didn't hesitate to pitch a picture-book idea at me. I still remember that it involved some multimedia musical tie-in and that it went on for a while. It was midnight and we had been in the hospital for twelve hours already, and I was too frazzled and freaked out to have the sense to shut her down."

That's desperation.

No sale.

There are many ways a writer can give off the scent of desperation. And believe me, agents and editors can pick up that scent from a distance of three hundred yards. When they smell it, they mentally spray themselves with repellent that puts up an instant protective shield.

Horror stories about inappropriate pitches are legion among editors.

Such as the limo driver who, instead of heading to the airport, went to a dark, empty lot, stopped, and insisted the editor read his screenplay. The editor thought she was going to be killed.

Or the editor who went to her sister's wedding rehearsal dinner and was seated between two priests. The one on the right pitched his children's story to her, while the one on the left kept insisting she had to publish it.

Or the slipped-under-the-bathroom-stall gambit that has happened more than once. I have an editor friend who is prepared for this. He says he will simply remove the first page and slip the manuscript back with this note scribbled on it: *Thank you. Your manuscript has met my needs at this time.*

Editors and agents want to deal with professionals. A professional is someone who knows the proper pitch and submission processes.

Act like a professional, and then you may become one.

The career novelist will develop a writing improvement program, beginning with a notebook.

You need to engage in something Geoff Colvin, in his book *Talent Is Overrated*, calls "deliberate practice."

What Colvin suggests is a rigorous program, usually designed by an expert teacher, that homes in on the most important areas of your endeavor, taking into account your particular needs, and designing training exercises.

These exercises must have a degree of difficulty, to take you out of your comfort zone.

Unless you're working with an expert instructor, you need to be designing your own writing improvement program.

One way to do that is with a Writing Improvement Notebook. Here are the sections I have in mine:

1. EXEMPLARS

Start with the authors you admire, the ones whose novels do the most for you. Find several paragraphs or pages in their books that really sing.

Make copies of these outstanding pages, and put them in this section.

Every now and again turn to one of these examples and write it out, word for word. Next, read the words out loud.

The idea is not to try to become an exact copy of the writer you admire. Rather, you are incorporating rhythms and possibilities into your own inner wiring. Your skill level will expand. You will grow as a writer.

2. OUTSIDE COMMENTS

In this section, record the comments you get from your critique group or your network of readers.

When you are published, keep copies of editorial letters and notes. These will remind you of areas in your writing you need to work on.

3. SELF STUDY

Work out a systematic plan to overcome your weak areas by setting up self-study programs.

For example, you might need one called "Creating Sympathetic Characters." Write out a specific thesis question:

How can I create characters that readers will bond with on an emotional level?

Next, make a list of all the novels you can think of where you really connected with the characters.

Select a handful of these novels and re-read them with the study question in mind. Underline passages that do the job and then *write some scenes where you try to do the same thing.*

This is not a word-for-word exercise. It's assimilating what works for others and filtering it through your own writer's mind.

Finally, buy some writing books that cover this area, or re-study some of the books you already own.

A writing notebook will increase your confidence, because every day you can be working on your craft, getting better. You'll feel it.

A writer must always be prepared to break through "the wall."

We all reach points in our writing that are like "the wall" marathon runners experience. It seems we can't go on, and we start to wonder if we ought to just scotch the whole writing thing. (To "scotch" means either to [a] give it up; or [b] drink it into oblivion. I recommend neither).

Be intentional about finding creative ways to bust through the wall. Here are a few of my own.

WRITE ANYTHING

Write something that is not your novel. Write a jingle for a commercial. A free-form poem about your car. A letter to the editor. Take inspiration from Malcolm Bradbury, in *Unsent Letters: Irreverent Notes From a Literary Life*:

> I write everything. I write novels and short stories and plays and playlets, interspersed with novellas and two-hander sketches. I write histories and biographies and introductions to the difficulties of modern science and cook books and books about the Loch Ness monster and travel

books, mostly about East Grinstead. ... I write children's books and school textbooks and works of abstruse philosophy ... and scholarly articles on the Etruscans and works of sociology and anthropology. I write articles for the women's page and send in stories about the most unforgettable characters I have ever met to *Reader's Digest*. ... I write romantic novels under a female pseudonym and detective stories ... I write traffic signs for the AA and "this side up" instructions for cardboard boxes. I believe I am really a writer.

BEHOLD IT

Ray Bradbury was writing the screenplay for John Huston's film version of *Moby-Dick*. With the script deadline looming, Bradbury was stuck. And increasingly desperate.

So he woke up one day and looked at himself in the mirror. "Behold, Herman Melville!" he said. Then he sat down and finished the script.

Take one of your favorite writers, preferably one who has written a book in your genre, look in the mirror, and say, "Behold, _____!"

Then sit down and write.

MAKE MUSIC

I play the ukulele. Badly. But I like it. It uses a different part of my brain, even though I'm not wired for music.

I strum "Yes Sir, That's My Baby" or "By the Light of the Silvery Moon," and ten minutes later, I'm ready to write again. Perhaps for no other reason than to shut myself up.

It works. Playing an instrument, even badly, fires off neurons of creativity in the brain.

EXERCISE

Take a nice, long walk. Don't think about your book. Have a little notebook or recorder with you.

You'll find the "boys in the basement" sending stuff up. When they do, write it down, and keep walking. (Note: I love Stephen King's metaphor of the "boys in the basement" from his book, *On Writing*. It refers to the writer's subconscious mind. Prompting the boys to do their work is one of the best ways to get through a wall.)

RANDOMIZE

Open a novel at random. Look at the first complete line on the left-hand page.

Put that line in your book, and start a scene with it.

After you've written the scene, cut the first line and substitute one of your own.

14

Turn envy into energy and more words.

Envy is a nasty beast that seems to haunt the lives of most writers. As Anne Lamott observes in *Bird by Bird*:

> ... If you continue to write, you are probably going to have to deal with [jealousy], because some wonderful, dazzling successes are going to happen for some of the most awful, angry, undeserving writers you know—people who are, in other words, not you.
>
> ...
>
> You are going to feel awful beyond words. You are going to have a number of days in a row where you hate everyone and don't believe in anything. If you do know the author whose turn it is, he or she will inevitably say that it will be your turn next, which is what the bride always says to you at each successive wedding, while you grow older and more decayed. It can wreak just the tiniest bit of havoc with your self-esteem to find that you are hoping for small bad things to happen to this friend—for, say, her head to blow up.

Envy has three sides.

The first is positive. It shows you care about your writing. If you don't have some emotions wrapped up in your enterprise, you're a zombie.

The second side is negative. It is an attack on your self-esteem. It messes with your insides and, at its worst, can keep you from writing.

The third side is poisonous. This form of envy is actually an undeserved attack on another person. This will diminish your humanity and make you a worse writer.

So when envy happens, acknowledge the good. You care about what you do.

> Every time a friend succeeds, I die a little.
>
> —Gore Vidal

But then, "Do not waste the remainder of thy life in thoughts about what other people are doing." That advice comes from Marcus Aurelius, a pretty good writer and emperor. You think he wasted time envying Epictetus?

Work and focus are what you need. If envy hits you hard, I'll allow you an hour to feel it for all it's worth. Call a friend or loved one and talk it out.

But after one hour, get back to the keyboard or writing pad and produce some words.

15

The successful novelist will not worry about competition, but will concentrate only on the page ahead.

You've just read something absolutely brilliant. It is original and fresh, written with such grace and style you're ready to weep. A mental voice kicks in: *I'll never write anything that brilliant. There is no way I can even approach this! Why try?*

I call this type of thinking the "Sam Snead Off the Practice Tee Syndrome."

Harvey Penick, the famous golf instructor, wanted to make a go at the professional tour. He worked and practiced and showed up at a tournament one day where he saw a kid hitting absolute rockets off the tee.

His jaw dropped as the kid hit blast after blast, sending the little white ball so straight and long that Penick knew, even on his best day, he could never come close to duplicating such prowess.

The kid's name was Sam Snead. Penick decided to become an instructor instead. A great one, too. He found his niche.

> In the end, a first-class you is better than a second-hand version of somebody else. Write books that can't be clumped with a bunch of similar ones.
>
> —David Morrell

But when it comes to writing, the "Sam Snead Off the Practice Tee Syndrome" is based on a fallacy.

When you read something that is stunningly original and think you could never, even on your best day, have thought that up, *you're right*. Nor could any other writer, anywhere.

That's because that particular bit of brilliance belongs to *that* writer alone. It came from his own mind and life and heart and experience, filtered through billions and billions of brain synapses over the course of decades. There is no way anyone else can duplicate that background.

And that's why there is more than one book published each year.

You have something unique to write, and your job is to find it.

Same goes for style. You have your own, waiting to get on the page.

And guess what? Mr. Brilliant Genius Writer cannot duplicate *you*.

So learn from the greats. Read and study those you admire. But never compare yourself to them.

You are becoming the best *you*, not another *them*.

Don't worry about trying to be better than someone else. Always try to be the very best *you* can be. Learn from others, yes. But don't just try to be better than they are. You have no control over that. Instead try, and try very hard, to be the best you can be. That you have control over.

—John Wooden, legendary
UCLA basketball coach

16

Don't worry about being worried, and don't let worry drag you down.

Not long after his novel *Hold Tight* debuted at #1 on the *New York Times* Best-Seller List, Harlan Coben was speaking to a crowd of suspense readers. He was asked if, with all his success, he still felt insecure with any part of his writing. He laughed and admitted that's the writer's stock in trade. Coben said he always gets to a point in a work-in-progress when he thinks, "This is terrible! I used to be so good. When did I lose it?"

In fact, if you're not insecure about your writing, Coben says, you're either mailing in forgettable stuff or somebody else is writing for you.

You will worry if you are a writer. Turn that worry into writing.

Some years ago, I was teaching at a writers' conference in New Mexico. After lunch I noticed one of the conferees sitting at a back table, looking distressed. I went over and asked her what was up.

"I don't know," she said. "Am I ever going to get anywhere? I see all these people; they all want it just as much as I do. How do I know if I'll ever make it?" Tears started down her cheeks. "Sorry," she said.

I handed her a paper napkin. Then I took another one and drew the following diagram:

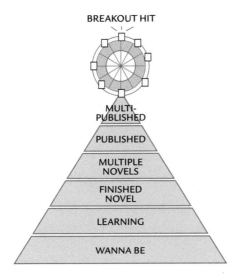

I explained that at the bottom, where most of the people are, is the realm of the "want to." Or "think I have a book inside me." But outside of some scribblings, maybe a short story or two, perhaps an unfinished novel, these people never move on to the next level ...

... which is where people like you are (I told her). Those who actually try to learn something about writing. Who buy writing books, go to conferences, take classes ... and write.

Above that is the level for those who actually finish a full-length novel. This is a great place to be. This is where *real writers* come from.

The next level holds those who write *another* novel, because the first one is probably going to be rejected. They do this, because they are novelists, not just someone who happened to write a novel.

Next are those who get published. Above that are those who are published multiple times.

At the very top is a Wheel of Fortune. This wheel goes around and lands on a book like *Cold Mountain*. Or *The Shack*. No one can control this.

Your job, I told the young woman, is to keep moving up the pyramid. Each level presents its own challenges, so concentrate on the ones right in front of you. As you move up, you'll notice there are fewer people, not more. If you work hard, you might get a novel on the wheel, and that's as far as you can get. After that, it's not up to you anymore.

The conference went on, and I eventually forgot all about this incident.

A couple of years later, I bumped into her at another conference. She told me that this conversation and the diagram had a profound effect on her, and that she was going to keep going.

Two years after that, she wrote to tell me she had landed a book deal. She is now a published author.

17

Stay hungry so your determination will not flag.

In the Stephen King short story, "All That You Love Will Be Carried Away," a traveling salesman pulls into a Motel 6 to commit suicide. Life on the road, the isolation of it, has caught up with him.

The only thing keeping him from eating a bullet is his odd journal, a collection of bathroom graffiti he has kept over the years. He thinks people will consider him crazy if they find the journal. He had once wanted to write a book about it.

You'll have to read the story, from the collection *Everything's Eventual*, to find out what happens. But it's one of King's best, with a haunting subtextual question: *What do we do when we see that which we love carried away?*

I've thought about this recently after some musings by a few of my novelist friends who are being dropped by their publishers for lack of sales. Or others who can't seem to land a new contract despite well-reviewed, award-winning novels.

Most writers think getting published is the key to the Kingdom. We have arrived in a literary Valhalla to take our place among the gods of print. Odin, looking like James Patterson, welcomes us with pints of mead and promises of immortality.

It's all an illusion, of course. There is no Valhalla. It's more like a dusty Barnes & Noble. And whatever shelf space we have can dry up in an instant. As General George S. Patton once put it, "All glory is fleeting."

I think my most joyful writing actually came before I was published. Partly it was ignorance—I didn't know how much I didn't know, and was just having fun putting down a story, letting it flow.

So happy was I that I wrote in my journal that I would always write, even if I never got published. Even if I had to print out copies at Kinko's and force them on my family at Thanksgiving and on perfect strangers outside Safeway.

Well, I did get published and it turned into a career, but that does not mean it's all roses, or that it might not go away sometime. No writer is fully immune from such thoughts.

So the question becomes what to do if it happens, if the publishers' doors slam?

I hope I would respond like one of my favorite writers, Preston Sturges. He was a blazing comet of success in the early 1940s, writing one great film comedy after another. He considered the possibility that all he had might be taken away and said, "When the last dime is gone, I'll sit on the curb with a pencil and a ten-cent notebook, and start the whole thing all over again."

Try to keep that attitude, no matter where your writing goes. If you get published, don't rest and think you've got it made. If the well dries up, don't stop.

18

An army travels on its stomach, so spear some fish.

Une armée marche à son estomac.

—Napoleon Bonaparte

You can't get an army to fight on inspiration alone. It has to be fed.

Nor can you wait for inspiration in your writing. As Jack London said, you have to "light out after it with a club." Which means, essentially, you have to become a walking idea factory.

And I do mean walking, because I get a lot of ideas when I'm doing moderate exercise.

I try to take an hour walk every day and listen to an audio book. Inevitably the "boys in the basement" send stuff up. I carry a small notebook and pen in my back pocket, and will stop and write down the ideas. Sometimes I record a memo on my phone. Whatever works.

Create a system for yourself that is "being creative without thinking about it." That way you can be "working" on your idea even when you're not working on it.

Follow these steps:

1. **RECORD.** Get fully focused on your idea during your writing time.

2. **TAKE A WALK.** You'll find ideas popping out at you. They're like fish in a stream. You are the ancient hunter-gatherer—only you spear the fish with your pen or pencil or keyboard or hand-held recorder. You make the meal later.

3. **THE MEAL.** I take my jottings or recordings and immediately put them into a document on my computer. I'll expand upon them, brainstorming outward from what I have. I'll do that with each idea until I'm done with the list.

4. **COOLING.** I wait until the next day to come back to the new ideas for assessment. This gives the boys a chance to work overnight while I'm sleeping.

5. **DECISION.** Remember, the way to get a brilliant idea is to come up with lots of ideas, then set aside the ones you don't use. Set them aside, but don't delete them. They may come in handy in another project entirely.

Get used to thinking this way, and your creativity will explode.

19

The fiction writer must rely on self-motivation.

The story is told of Sun Tzu being challenged by a king to train 180 women, including his two favorite concubines, into an orderly company. Sun Tzu accepted, and put the two concubines in command of the troops.

But when Sun Tzu started giving orders, the company of women started giggling. Sun Tzu tried again. Same result.

This failure to obey, Sun Tzu claimed, was the fault of the commanders. So he ordered the two concubines beheaded.

That seemed to get everyone's attention. There was no more laughter.

Now that's motivation.

All writers need it, but I wouldn't go so far as Sun Tzu on this one. Sure, negative motivation, like a mortgage payment, can be good for producing words.

But I prefer the more positive kind.

In my office, I have pictures of three writers I admire.

The first picture is of Stephen King, in his home office, feet up on the desk, looking over a manuscript. He's dressed casually. His dog is under his legs, looking at the camera. This is my idea of good working conditions.

Then there's a picture of John D. MacDonald, tapping away at his typewriter, pipe in mouth. He was prolific (his biography is aptly titled *Red Hot Typewriter*) and a great storyteller and stylist.

The photo reminds me to keep producing words.

Finally, I have a picture of Evan Hunter/Ed McBain, from the back of one of his novels, arms folded, staring out as if in challenge. He was even more prolific than MacDonald, writing both literary and genre novels.

If I'm not working hard enough, he reminds me to get going again.

Create your own stock of visual motivators. Put them where you write. Look at them when you don't feel like writing, but know you must.

20

A gentle reminder can deliver great force at just the right time.

It's the little things that mount up to victory. So make yourself a reminder list, changing it periodically as you grow in your writing skill.

I put my reminders on little Post-it notes stuck on a 5 × 8 card. That way I can easily revise them.

Currently, here are the notes on my card:

> Emotion, emotion, emotion!
>
> Be dialogue happy.
>
> The right answer.
>
> Surprise me now!

Here's what those notes mean:

EMOTION, EMOTION, EMOTION!

This reminds me that the primary objective of a novel is to give the reader an emotional ride. If I get too analytical and lose the heart, I have to stop and start a fire inside me, then inside the characters.

BE DIALOGUE HAPPY.

Let the dialogue flow. I can always edit it later.

THE SECOND RIGHT ANSWER.

Learn to stop at every major creative decision and go to the *next* "right answer." My brain usually feeds me a cliché, the standard, the same old. So I make a list of alternatives and choose one of these.

SURPRISE ME NOW!

Whenever the story even holds the hint of dragging, I want to create a surprise. Something to beef up the narrative. Like the old Raymond Chandler trick of just bringing in a guy with a gun. Any variation on that theme.

What are your most important reminders? Make that list now, and start using it.

1. _____

2. _____

3. _____

4. _____

Put heart into everything you write.

A highly successful author once told David Morrell that he chose his genre by pure market calculation. And it worked for him. Which is fine. In our free enterprise system, that's permissible.

Morrell, after hearing this, reflected that he is just not constituted to be that kind of writer. He can write only when there is something (an "inner ferret," he calls it) gnawing at him, something that needs expression from the deepest part of himself.

I like to see a writer's heart on the page.

Heart = passion + purpose.

Passion means heat. Strength of feeling.

Purpose means you know what you want the reader to feel when she gets to the end of your story.

Heart means directing passion so it serves your desired purpose.

Leon Uris once said, "You have to evolve a permanent set of values to serve as motivation." His books have sold more than 150 million copies worldwide and have been translated into twenty-nine languages.

Why?

Uris was a Marine in World War II, and his lead characters are often involved in grand battles for justice. *Battle Cry, Exodus, QB VII*, and *Trinity* reached the top spot on the *New York Times* Best-Seller List because Uris's heart was evident in the stories.

Consider also two novels published in 1957, both of which became bestsellers and, to this day, sell tens of thousands of copies per year.

Yet they couldn't be more different.

On the Road by Jack Kerouac is a book-length jazz riff celebrating present-moment experience.

Atlas Shrugged by Ayn Rand is a monumental door-stop of a novel that is a philosophical argument for the life of the mind and "rational self-interest."

So what accounts for the perennial popularity of these two divergent novels?

Three things.

First, they were *about* something. For Kerouac, this journey on the road was the pursuit of "beatitude" (the word Kerouac insisted was the real basis for the word "Beat").

Rand wanted nothing less than to shift the entire course of Western Civilization. (No pressure.)

Second, the authors believed what they were writing. You can't read a single page in these books that does not contain personal narrative fervor.

Finally, they cared about their craft. They had two entirely different styles, of course. But both worked hard to get good at what they did. Rand wrote in the grand romantic tradition of Victor Hugo. Kerouac was trying to develop a whole new approach he called "Be Bop Prose Rhapsody." Both succeeded in their unique fashion.

To pinpoint your passion:

1. Start by making a list of all the things you believe most strongly.

2. Now make a list of your all-time favorite books and movies, and describe how each one of them made you feel at the end.

3. When you start looking for that next novel idea, select one item from each list and brainstorm on how you might combine them in a story. Determine never to write another novel you don't have your heart in.

22

Finish your novel, because you learn more that way than any other.

Some writers tinker over their words endlessly, perhaps fearing the end result. It might stink.

Yes, it might, but it's the only way you're going to get better.

Finish your novel.

> In war, then, let your great object be victory, not lengthy campaigns.
>
> —Sun Tzu

part II
TACTICS

Water shapes its course according to the nature of the ground over which it flows; the soldier works out his victory in relation to the foe whom he is facing. Therefore, just as water retains no constant shape, so in warfare there are no constant conditions. He who can modify his tactics in relation to his opponent and thereby succeed in winning, may be called a heaven-born captain.

—Sun Tzu

Write. Remember, people may keep you (or me) from being a published author but no one can stop you from being a writer. All you have to do is write. And keep writing. While you're working at a career, while you're raising children, while you're trout fishing—keep writing! No one can stop you but you.

—Katherine Neville

The writer of potential greatness settles not for "mere fiction."

A couple of years ago some writer friends and I were discussing the merits of *Moby-Dick*. As I recall, only one other intrepid soul joined me in extolling the virtues of Herman Melville's classic. The language is like the ocean itself, I opined, with highs and lows and storms and calms. (One of the other writers thought this sounded more like a Harlequin romance scene than a description of the book, but I digress.)

It turns out that the loudest howls of protest came from those who had been forced to read *Moby-Dick* in school. Not many kids are ready for that. I was lucky to read *Moby-Dick* for the first time after college, just because I wanted to. I loved it. (As an aside, if you do decide to give the book a try, or *another* try, be sure to pick up a version with illustrations by Rockwell Kent. They are the perfect meeting of artist and novel.)

I do think there is one point the critics and supporters of *Moby-Dick* can agree upon, and that is this: Melville can never be accused of writing *mere fiction*. He was *going for it*. In sports parlance, he was leaving it all out there on the floor. Herm could have made a good living writing penny dreadfuls, but he was after more than a living. He was about that elusive dream of literature as apotheosis. He was himself pursuing a white whale of artistic vision. God love him.

By the way, that term *mere fiction* comes from an essay by the late John Gardner, the noted novelist, teacher and essayist. I like the term, because there is too little time for anyone to be settling for mere fiction.

> While heeding the profit of my counsel, avail yourself also of any helpful circumstances over and beyond the ordinary rules.
>
> —Sun Tzu

So I was roundly castigated in the group for daring to enjoy *Moby-Dick*. This went on for some time.

I had to laugh, then, when a couple of days after what I now call "The Great Moby Dustup," I picked up my copy of *'Salem's Lot* by Stephen King. I'd read it years ago, but my son got me the new, illustrated hardback edition for Christmas. And it had a new introduction by the author.

At this point in his career, King was still an unpublished novelist. *Carrie* had yet to come out. But he had this vision for a vampire book that was breathtaking in its grandiosity, especially for a twenty-three-year-old without a novel on the shelf. He wanted to combine, he says, the vampire myth of Bram Stoker's *Dracula* with the "naturalistic fiction of Frank Norris and the EC horror comics I'd loved as a child ... . Did I really think I could combine *Dracula* and *Tales From the Crypt* and come out with *Moby-Dick*? I did. I really did ... . Was I daunted by the fact that *Moby-Dick* only sold about twelve copies in Melville's lifetime? Not I; one of my ideas was that a novelist takes the long view, the *lofty* view, and that does not include the price of eggs. (My wife would not have agreed, and I doubt if Mrs. Melville would have, either.)"

Well bravo for King. And Melville. No mere fiction for these two. And look! Melville, forgotten in his lifetime, is still talked about today and taught in college courses. King himself is taught *right now*, and has sold considerably more than twelve copies.

Which is to say, *go for it*. Don't settle for mere fiction.

Have a little of the twenty-three-year-old Stephen King 'tude. You won't fail. As the old advertising man Leo Burnett once said, "When you reach for the stars you may not quite get one, but you won't come up with a handful of mud either."

A writer with a credo will not be tempted to settle for mediocrity.

It was W. Somerset Maugham who famously stated, "There are three rules for writing a novel. Unfortunately, no one knows what they are." This is often quoted in writing classes to give the huddled scribes comfort as they approach the mysterious alchemy that is fiction writing.

Well, far be it from me to take on Mr. Maugham, but perhaps I can offer at least three *essentials* for a successful novel.

I took them from the credo of one of my favorite writers, John D. MacDonald. He wrote a series of amazingly good (and diverse) paperbacks in the '50s, then created an enduring series characters, Travis McGee. His output was prodigious, but his essentials remained the same.

In *Revision & Self-Editing*, I gave the credo. Here I would like to comment upon it.

Essential #1

First, there has to be a strong sense of story. I want to be intrigued by wondering what is going to happen next. I want the people that I read about to be in difficulties—emotional, moral, spiritual, whatever, and I want to live with them while they're finding their way out of these difficulties.

—John D. MacDonald

Notice what MacDonald meant by story. The reader has to wonder what is going to happen next. To *people*. That creates the page-turning effect, and it applies not just to commercial fiction but literary as well.

Remember Alfred Hitchcock's axiom: "A good story is life, with the dull parts taken out."

No trouble for intriguing people = dull.

So we might sum up the first essential this way: Create characters readers will be drawn to and put them in desperate straits *soon*.

Essential #2

Second, I want the writer to make me suspend my disbelief; I want to be in some other place and scene of the writer's devising.

—John D. MacDonald

Simply put, we must weave a dreamscape for the readers. We have to create the impression of something really happening in a real world to real people. That's as true for fantasy as it is reality-based fiction.

Readers *want* to suspend their disbelief. They start out on your side. They hope your words will lift them out of their lives and into another realm.

So how do you do this? First, by being *accurate*. If you're writing about 1905 Los Angeles, do not include the Dodgers. Or if you're writing about lawyers, don't have one asking his own witness leading questions without the other side objecting. And so on. You have to know your world before you write about it.

One way to get it right is through experts. People love to talk about what they do, if you approach them correctly.

Get into research. Some writers, like a James Michener, do a ton of research up front. Others, like Stephen King, wait until the first draft is done and then see what needs to be fleshed out.

I like a method in between. Enough research to write knowingly, then when I come to a place in my book that needs detail or depth, I'll leave a comment in my document and pick a time later to research it more. I do this so I don't end up writing a long scene that is completely off-base.

And always choose the *telling detail* over *plain vanilla description*.

"He jumped into his car and drove away."

Wait. What kind of car was it?

"She was beautiful."

Was she? I don't believe it. Describe her so I'll know it. Show me how other characters react to her.

Essential #3

> Next, I want [the writer] to have a bit of magic in his prose style, a bit of unobtrusive poetry. I want to have words and phrases really sing.
>
> —John D. MacDonald

The key word here is *unobtrusive*. If the prose stands out too much, shouting "Look at me! I'm wonderful writing!" the suspension of disbelief takes a hit.

But if it's dull, if it moves the story along like a burro in Calexico, it creates no magic.

A lot of the examples I like come from the hard-boiled tradition. Such as Robert B. Parker's *Pale Kings and Princes*:

> The sun that brief December day shone weakly through the west-facing window of Garrett Kingsley's office. It made a thin yellow oblong splash on his Persian carpet and gave up.

Or John D. MacDonald's *Darker Than Amber*:

> She sat up slowly, looked in turn at each of us, and her dark eyes were like twin entrances to two deep caves. Nothing lived in those caves. Maybe something had, once upon a time. There were piles of bones back in there, some scribbling on the walls, and some gray ash where the fires had been.

Or Dennis Lehane's *Darkness, Take My Hand*:

> He's pretty silly-looking—a gangly, tall guy
> with hips like doorknobs and unruly, brittle hair
> that looks like he styles it by sticking his head in a
> toilet bowl and flushing.

Fiction of a more literary style is usually built on a foundation of unobtrusive poetry.

In John Fante's *Ask the Dust*, the would-be writer Arturo Bandini has severe writer's block, typing only two words in two days, *palm tree*, because a palm tree is outside his window:

> [A] battle to the death between the palm tree
> and me, and the palm tree won: see it out there
> swaying in the blue air, creaking sweetly in the blue
> air. The palm tree won after two fighting days, and
> I crawled out of the window and sat at the foot
> of the tree. Time passed, a moment or two, and
> I slept, little brown ants carousing in the hair on
> my legs.

The repeated phrase *blue air* is ironic and mocking, like everything Bandini comes across in his quest for success. And the word *carousing* completes the passage—this celebration of ants mocking a young writer's pain.

I'm sure you have your own favorites. The question is, how do you get this sort of thing in your own writing?

Say you want to describe someone's wild hair. Write for five minutes without stopping. Describe the hair in two hundred or three hundred words. Let the images a fly. Go back later and find the good parts and edit them down.

In fact, the right brain/left brain dynamic is crucial here. Find ways to write without the infamous inner editor constantly shutting you down. Write hot, revise cool.

And read some poetry. Ray Bradbury used to read poetry every day. The lilt of the language will help you tap into different parts of your writer's brain.

25

Write hard, write fast, and the fire of creation will be yours.

Not long ago, I got an e-mail from a young writer:

> Did I tell you I signed up for NaNoWriMo [National Novel Writing Month]? It has been a challenge, but I'm making the word count. I have discovered something interesting about this seat-of-the-pants writer, this system works for me!!! I have a touch of OCD so when I write a rough draft, I tend to revise it into oblivion before the first draft is done. With NaNo I am forced to forge ahead with the story. I love it.

Forging ahead with the story allows it to live and breathe and take on new life.

So when you write that first draft, my advice is: Write hard, write fast.

Revise the previous day's writing, then move ahead with what's in front of you.

That's it. As fast as you comfortably can, until the first draft is done.

I contend that new writers would actually improve their craft—and chances of getting published—if they would write faster, especially at the beginning of their learning curve. Here's why.

First, you learn most about writing a full-length novel by actually writing a full-length novel. It is much more valuable to do this repeatedly than to hover too long over one unfinished (or unpolished) manuscript.

Second, you become a professional in the best sense of the word (well, maybe second-best sense, the first-best being *getting paid*). A professional is someone who does his job, every day, even if he doesn't feel like it. A surgeon can't refuse to operate because he's upset over the Laker game last night. A criminal defense lawyer can't ask for a continuance so he can go to the beach and dream of someday getting a client who is actually innocent.

And a professional writer can't sit at the computer playing Spider Solitaire, waiting for a visit from the Muse. A pro is someone who writes, whether inspired or not, and keeps on writing.

I've counseled many writers at conferences who have come with a single manuscript yet haven't got another project going. I tell them, "That's wonderful. You've written a novel. That's a great accomplishment. Now, get to work on the next one. And as you're writing that next one, be developing an idea for the project after that."

Publishers and agents invest in careers. They want to know you can do this over and over again.

Some of the best novels of the past century were produced at a rapid clip by authors who found writing time each day, and simply went at their task with singular resolution:

- William Faulkner wrote *As I Lay Dying* in six weeks, writing from midnight to 4 A.M., then sending it off to the publisher without changing a word. (You're not Faulkner, by the way.)

- Ernest Hemingway wrote what some consider his best novel, *The Sun Also Rises*, also in six weeks, part of it in Madrid, and the last of it in Paris, in 1925.

- In one stunning stretch (1953–1954) John D. MacDonald produced seven novels of high quality. Over the course of the decade, he wrote many more superb books, including the classic *The End of the Night*, which some mention in the same breath as Truman Capote's *In Cold Blood*. Also *Cry Hard, Cry Fast*, which is the basis for the title of this entry.

  So prolific was MacDonald that he was needled by a fellow writer who, over martinis, sniffed that John should slow down, ignore "paperback drivel," and get to "a real novel." MacDonald sniffed back that in thirty days he could write a novel that would be published in hardback, serialized in the magazines, selected by a book club, and turned into a movie. The other writer laughed and bet him $50 that he couldn't pull it off.

MacDonald went home and, in a month, wrote *The Executioners*. It was published in hardback by Simon & Schuster, serialized in a magazine, selected by a book club, and turned into the movie *Cape Fear*. Twice.

- Ray Bradbury famously wrote his classic *Fahrenheit 451* in nine days on a rented typewriter. "I had a newborn child at home," he recalls, "and the house was loud with her cries of exaltation at being alive. I had no money for an office, and while wandering around UCLA I heard typing from the basement of Powell Library. I went to investigate and found a room with twelve typewriters that could be rented for ten cents a half hour. So, exhilarated, I got a bag of dimes and settled into the room, and in nine days I spent $9.80 and wrote my story; in other words, it was a dime novel."

- Jack London was anything but promising as a young writer. He could hardly string sentences together in a rudimentary fashion. About all he had was desire. He shut himself up in a room and wrote. Daily. Sometimes eighteen hours a day. He sent stories off that got returned. He filled up a trunk with rejections. But all the time he was learning, learning. When he died at the age of forty, he was one of the most prolific and successful writers of all time.

- John O'Hara wrote fast, and well, turning out books, stories and plays over the course of his long career.

- Charles Dickens wrote fast. He had to. He had ten children. And he wrote many of his novels in installments for literary magazines. He had to keep the chapters coming.

- Stephen King says he used to write 1,500 words a day, every day, except his birthday and the 4th of July. A prodigious output resulting in the National Book Award Medal of Distinguished Contribution to American Letters.

One could go on, but the lesson is clear. Writing "genius," like any other kind, is 99 percent perspiration. These authors all worked extremely hard early in their careers to learn their craft. By writing relatively fast, they forced themselves to learn. Their books were not the product of small bits of inspiration, but rather steady, dedicated, intense work, day after day.

I do have writer friends who believe that writing slowly, carefully, polishing as they go, is the best way to produce quality work. That's fine for them. It may even be fine for you.

But I urge you to consider the idea of "the zone" that comes when you write your story quickly, intensely. Take time with your "pre-writing," whatever form that takes for you. Then follow the advice of Dorothea Brande, from her little classic *Becoming a Writer*:

> Say to yourself: "At ten o'clock on Wednesday I will begin to write [the story]," and then dismiss it from your mind. Now and then it will rise to the surface. You need not reject it with violence, but reject it. You are not ready for it yet; let it subside again. Three days will do it no harm, will even help it. But when ten o'clock strikes on Wednesday you sit down to work.
>
> Now; strike out at once. ... [T]ake no excuses, refuse to feel any stage fright; simply start working. If a good first sentence does not come, leave a space for it and write it in later. Write as rapidly as possible, with as little attention to your own processes as you can give.

I interviewed Steve Martini and asked about his approach, and he said, "My manuscripts, which are fairly long (130,000 to 150,000 words), are produced in final form in a period of between four and five months. For this reason my writing day is very long and often stretches from late morning until late into the night and as the deadline approaches often into the wee hours of the morn-

战82争

ing. It can be very intense, but I find that plots that are intricate and involved with numerous twists are often best crafted in a more compressed time frame. It's easier to retain mastery over all of the complex story elements."

Isaac Asimov, author/editor of seven hundred-plus books, was once asked what he would do if he knew he had only six months to live.

"Type faster," he said.

Edit slow, edit tough,
with a process both clear
and cool.

It's in the editing phase that you slow down, see what you have, and make it better.

Having written a book on the process of revision I won't repeat the material here. I will say that there does come a point of *diminishing returns*. You can workshop or critique group something to death and reach a place where it isn't improving.

At some point you have to send it out.

How do you know what that point is?

Create a process, a schedule, a checklist for yourself. (You'll find many suggestions for this in *Revision & Self-Editing*.)

Make this process as clear as possible. Maybe it includes sending your manuscript to several test readers, and if the majority of them like it, you go for it. If you get the same criticism from more than one reader, fix it and then go for it.

Maybe it means using Sol Stein's idea of triage as explained in his *Stein on Writing*. This is a good strategy, too, wherein you tackle the most important fixes first.

There's no one way to approach your editing. The important thing is to make *a way* for yourself and then, gasp, follow it as if you were a bomb inspector going through the standard routine.

Every time.

27

Test your premise to prove it worthy.

Editors and agents are all looking for the "same thing," only "different."

That's the elusive marketing angle that tells them: a) we can sell this because similar books have sold before; but b) there's a freshness to it.

So how do you create this fusion?

It all starts with your *premise*. Which is another way of saying your *big idea*.

When you come up with an idea for a novel, write it down in a dedicated file or document. Collect possible story ideas the way a kid might collect autumn leaves or sea shells. Whatever you think up, toss into a file.

Eventually, you'll need to decide which premise you're going to develop and turn into a book.

Sort through all of your ideas and choose the ones you like best. I put my favorite ideas into another file I call "Front Burner Concepts." These are the ones I think have the most potential. I go over these frequently, rearranging the order, adding new ones, dropping others.

Then I have to get to the decision point. Which concept am I going to spend the next several months turning into a novel?

Try to push your "front burner" premises through the following filter.

1. Is your Lead character someone you can see and hear? If not:

   - Cast the character. Really "see" him.

   - Do some dialogue where the Lead introduces himself to you.

2. Does your Lead character have heroic qualities, either evident or potential? Define them.

3. Who is the Opposition, and how is this character stronger than the Lead?

4. How is "death overhanging"? (Is it physical, professional, psychological? All three?)

5. Can you see a climactic battle, won by the Lead?

6. Can you envision a possible inner journey?

   - Begin at the end. Because of the climactic action, how will the Lead grow?

   - Or, at the very least, consider this: What will the Lead have learned that is essential to his humanity?

Example: At the end of *Lethal Weapon*, Riggs gives up the bullet he's saved to shoot himself.

He has learned that life is worth living and that love from friends is worth accepting.

7. Take a break.

   - During this break, do you find yourself thinking about your Lead character? Not your plot, your Lead. Is she starting to become real to you? And, most important, are you beginning to care enough about her to give her a story? Do you feel her story has to be written?

   - When you wake up in the morning, are you still juiced about the Lead and the story?

8. Do a cold-hearted market analysis of your idea.

   - Who will want to read this story, and why?

   - Will the answer to the first question be enough for a publisher to publish your book? (Be honest.)

   - Can you truly see browsers in a store picking up your book and wanting to buy it?

   - Write a one-paragraph description of your idea. Read this to several trusted friends and ask for their reactions. If they love it, great. If they shake their heads, find out why. Make any changes you deem necessary.

9. Write a short e-mail to yourself, as if you were a reader writing to a friend about what was so great about this book. How did it make you feel? What gripped you about it? You can do this in general terms, but it must be enough to make you want that book to see the light of day.

10. Put all this away for one week. During this week, work on steps 1 through 9 with a different idea. Then come back to your original premise and see if you are still excited about it, if it still "calls out to you" to be written. If so, start developing it in earnest.

In this way, you can, in very short order, have several possible novel ideas cooking at any one time. Eventually, you'll choose the one you are going to push through to the end. That's always a tough call! But this process is much better than grabbing your first premise and charging ahead. Much time may be wasted this way.

Ever since I started writing professionally, I told myself I have only a finite time on this earth and can only write a finite number of books. I need to choose the best ones for me and for my readers both. This is the method I use to do that.

The fully engaged writer must extend operations to the two levels of story.

There are two levels of story. Various terms are used to describe them, but, for shorthand, I'll use Outer and Inner.

The Outer level (sometimes called *plot*) is a record of the events that happen to and around the main character.

The Inner level (sometimes referred to as *story*) is the record of what happens *inside* the character as a result of the plot.

When you are outlining your novel, or drafting your scene ideas, or simply brainstorming, give equal thought to both aspects.

Here are more terms to describe the two levels:

> Outer: action
> Inner: reaction
> Outer: motion
> Inner: emotion
> Outer: goal
> Inner: growth
> Outer: attain
> Inner: become

How much emphasis you give to each level in your story depends on what kind of novel you're writing. Generally, the character-driven story pays closer attention to inner growth, while a plot-driven story is more action oriented. But within these general parameters is a wide swath for you to determine exactly how you want the story to feel to the reader.

In your pre-writing, deepen your Lead's inner journey by answering the following questions:

1. Who does the Lead need to be at the end of the novel in order to be "whole"?

2. Why is it important for the Lead to be whole in this way? What "life lesson" does it teach?

3. Where is the Lead now (broken)? Describe.

4. Why is the Lead this way? (Look to the past.)

5. Has the past created a "wound"? How does the wound manifest itself in the present (behaviors, attitudes, reactions)?

6. What is preventing the Lead from being whole?

7. How will the Lead be forced to change (or refuse to change)?

8. What must the Lead sacrifice to become whole?

9. What final scene or image will prove the change?

Let's take a familiar example: Rick, played by Humphrey Bogart in *Casablanca*.

1. At the end of the film, in order to be whole, Rick must rejoin the larger community—his country and its war effort.

2. The lesson is clear. No man is an island (a familiar theme when you have an antihero, which is what Rick is).

3. The Lead is in the desert (literally) running a saloon, sticking his neck out for nobody, and not even caring if he dies ("Go ahead and shoot," he tells Ilsa at one point. "You'll be doing me a favor.").

4. Rick is this way because the woman he loved most in the world betrayed him (or so he thinks).

5. This wound manifests itself in Rick not caring what happens to others, in too much drink, in cynicism about everything.

6. Rick is prevented from changing because there is no one who can truly reach him. Not even his friend, Sam. Or the women with whom he has occasional flings.

7. Rick will be forced to change, or to resist change, when Ilsa shows up in Casablanca with Victor

Laszlo, and Rick's help is the only way those two can escape the clutches of the Nazis.

8. Rick sacrifices his own happiness. Ilsa has agreed to leave with him but he insists she get on the plane with Victor, and even puts his own life on the line by shooting the Nazi, Major Strasser.

9. In the final shot, Rick goes off with his new friend, Captain Renault, to rejoin the war effort. He has been resurrected. The antihero comes back to the community.

No matter what kind of novel you write, attention paid to both levels of story will elevate your manuscript above a mountain of slush passing before the bleary eyes of agents and editors.

29

Disdain not the freshness of small improvements outside comfort zones.

If you are a "character-driven" writer, spend an extra 10 percent of your writing time ratcheting up the action. How can the events of the story be made more threatening, suspenseful, fresh?

If you are more on the "plot-driven" side, spend 10 percent of your writing time going deeper into the emotions of the character, how she is reacting to the events, how they threaten her inner well-being.

And when you do this 10 percent exercise be sure to push yourself and go beyond what's comfortable. Well beyond. Because *you can always scale it back later.* But if you don't allow yourself the fullness of exploration up front, you may miss the rich vein waiting for you just a few more steps ahead.

Now, open up a new document or take out a pad and write for five minutes without stopping. Write a list of what can happen that's *worse*, letting the thoughts come fast and furious. Don't edit. Be as outrageous as you can be.

Then stop, walk around for a couple of minutes, and come back and choose the idea you like best. Rewrite the scene now. Repeat the process for several other scenes.

For you plot-driven people, find a place in your manuscript where something bad has happened to your Lead (there should be lots of these places!). Now, open a new document or write on a pad for five minutes using the voice journal method (see "The use of a voice journal will keep characters from becoming little versions of the writer." on page 116). Write down the character's inner thoughts as passionately as you can, in his own words. Keep pressing for more depth.

Then stop, walk around for a couple of minutes, and sit down and highlight the best portions. Rewrite the scene, incorporating these insights as the character's thoughts, bits of dialogue or narration.

30

The key to reader bonding is falling in love with the Lead.

Plot alone won't get the job done. Twists and turns and chases and guns won't do it.

For your novel to blast off, your readers have to fall in love with your Lead character.

As a reminder, there are three types of Leads: positive, negative, and antihero.

Positive refers to the traditional hero, who represents the values of the community. We root for him because when he wins, we all win. Our collective sense of morality is vindicated.

A *negative* Lead, as the name implies, is doing things we don't approve of. If he succeeds, it's bad news because others might follow him.

The *antihero* operates according to his own moral code. He has left the community. The story may draw him back in for a time, and then he will have a decision to make. Does he stay or go back to being alone?

A reader can fall in love with any of these types.

We love the positive because we're on his side; the antihero because we like individualists. But what about the negative Lead?

Think about forbidden love. Usually that is manifested through power. We are drawn to powerful negative Leads, especially if they have a little charm. We have a part inside us that wonders what it would be like to have such power.

All that said, here are the things you need to know to get readers loving your Leads.

1. Great Leads have grit, wit, and it. *Grit* is guts. Courage. Inner strength. A Lead needs it, or needs to develop it over the course of the story.

Wit is mental acuity, usually laced with a little humor. A Lead needs wit to get through the thicket of the many confrontations in the plot.

It is what they used to call "sex appeal." It's based on inner energy. Clara Bow, the silent screen actress, was dubbed the "It Girl" in the twenties. Onscreen, she generated an insouciance and self-possession that women admired and men found irresistible. Your Lead needs to have an inner *something* that would make anyone want to know what makes her tick.

2. Character is revealed in crisis. We learn about Scarlett O'Hara when the Civil War breaks out. She is forced to deal with hardships (challenging her selfishness) and has the strength to do so.

Michael Corleone starts on the road to becoming the Godfather when his own father is almost killed.

So pile on the tests and let us see how they reveal the insides of your Lead.

3. You should know your Lead's deepest thoughts, yearnings, secrets, and fears. And you should know this early in the writing process.

Some authors like to create extensive biographies. I have always found this tough slogging. What I prefer is the voice journal (see page 116). I just allow my characters to talk, in stream-of-consciousness mode, and type what I hear them say. Like I'm interviewing them, and allowing them to open up.

4. Emotionally bond the reader to the Lead character. Some ways to do this are:

1. Make the Lead care about someone other than himself.

2. Have the Lead do things to help those weaker than he is (this is also known as the "pet the dog" beat). Here's an example from the TV series *Mad Men*:

    Don Draper, the skirt-chasing Lead, gets on an elevator with a couple of other guys. The two guys are talking in a sexually explicit way. A woman gets on the elevator. The two guys keep up the uncivil chatter. Draper notices the woman is uncomfortable.

To the loudest mouth, Draper says, "Take off your hat."

The guy says, "Excuse me?"

"Take off your hat." Draper takes the hat off the guy and shoves it in his chest.

A small beat, but it gave this complex character some needed nobility when it counted. And another great point about this is that Draper didn't make some clichéd speech about manners. He just *showed* who he was by what he did.

3. Put the Lead in a situation of jeopardy, hardship or vulnerability.

Do these things, and you will be at least 75 percent of the way toward a novel readers won't want to put down.

31

Deploy a character who reveals both inner struggle and inner conflict.

An *inner struggle* is something the Lead brings with her into the story. It's there before the narrative begins. It's the struggle that is holding her back in life itself, not just in the plot.

The *inner conflict* is a product of the plot. It is the "argument" the character is having inside over pursuit of the objective.

Here's how to get at these elements.

INNER STRUGGLE

First, figure out what the most positive characteristic of your Lead is. What do you want the readers to know most about her after they've finished the novel?

Let's say you choose *determined*. Now, list what battles against that characteristic. *Timidity* perhaps, or *hesitancy*.

Next, create in your Lead's background a reason for this struggle. Maybe it was something from her childhood, a traumatic incident of some kind. Or the way she was raised. Or someone she looked up to telling her she'd never amount to anything in life. Dramatize this, and you can well use the beat as a "reveal" in your novel.

Remember, inner struggle is not tied to the plot. It's something the Lead *brings* to the plot from her past, and it is something she will carry with her throughout the story. The pressures of the plot will put her in places where she has to somehow deal with this struggle.

It may be that she's just fighting herself. But eventually, she's going to have to choose which of the two sides she will let control her.

This exercise will automatically, and without a great deal of effort, transform your Leads from plain vanilla to dynamic and dimensional.

INNER CONFLICT

Inner conflict is related to the plot. It springs from the Lead's objective.

He has to get—or get away from—something, and the realization of this goal is essential to his well-being. Death overhangs: If he does not achieve the objective, he will die—physically, professionally, and/or psychologically.

But as the forces gather against him, there is another "voice" inside, arguing that he must give up. It may be the voice of pure fear. Or the simple realization of his limitations and the odds he's up against.

These two sides put him on the rack emotionally, as long as you make the case for each as strong as possible.

Another exercise:

Write a page-long passage, with heightened intensity, revealing the inner struggle.

Then write another passage, this time revealing the inner conflict.

Feel the hot tongs of emotion as you write.

Then see if you can find a place in your novel to place these beats. You can edit them down, of course, to fit your needs. But try to use both of them somewhere, in some form.

Here is the way Mickey Spillane revealed the inside of his P.I. Mike Hammer in *One Lonely Night*:

> So the judge was right all the while. I could feel the madness in my brain eating its way through my veins, chewing the edges of my nerves raw, leaving me something that resembled a man and that was all. *The judge had been right!* There *had* been too many of those dusks and dawns; there *had* been a pleasure in all that killing, an obscene pleasure that froze your face in a grin even when you were charged with fear. ... I enjoyed that killing, every bit of it. I killed because I had to and I killed things that needed killing. But that wasn't the point. *I enjoyed killing those things and I knew the judge was right!* I was rotten right through and I knew that at that moment my face was twisted out of shape into a grin that was half sneer and my heart beat fast because it was nice sitting back there with a rod under my arm and somebody was going to hurt pretty quick now, then die. And it

might even be me and I didn't give a good damn
one way or another.

Inner struggle and inner conflict will ratchet up the emotional experience for your readers and strengthen their bond with your characters.

32

The writer who understands redemption is on the border of enduring fiction.

Many great stories are about a character's redemption—or the failure to redeem a character. This aspect can lend real power to an otherwise standard plot.

In *A Man for All Seasons* the thematic-redemptive thread is in the Richard Rich character. He is given a clear moral choice, and chooses to give false witness against Sir Thomas More for a chance to rule in Wales. (I love the way Paul Scofield delivers that devastating line to Rich in the film, "Why Richard, it profits a man nothing to give his soul for the whole world ... but for Wales?"). The Thomas More character is given the mirror image choice to give up his principles, and refuses.

In the film *The Fugitive*, it is not Richard Kimble (Harrison Ford) but Sam Gerard (Tommy Lee Jones) who is offered redemption, and takes it. He goes from being the lawman who says, "I don't care!" (about the facts, that's not his job) to caring for and saving Kimble. "Don't tell anybody," he says to Kimble at the end.

Flannery O'Connor talked about the need of a story to show "grace being offered." So it can be either the

Lead who is offered redemption, or another character for whom the Lead is the catalyst for redemption. Let's see how this works.

- *Braveheart*: It's Robert the Bruce who is redeemed by William Wallace's death.

- *The Godfather*: Michael (Lead) is offered redemption (when his wife asks him to tell her the truth) and refuses it by lying to her face.

- *One Flew Over the Cuckoo's Nest*: Chief Broom is redeemed via McMurphy.

- *Tootsie*: Michael (Lead) is redeemed because he's learned how to treat women as human beings.

- *Casablanca*: The Lead, Rick, is redeemed when he decides to rejoin the war effort and get out of Casablanca, where he had gone to drink himself to death.

- *Sunset Boulevard*: Joe Gillis is redeemed, but too late (one definition of tragedy).

Redemption is bound up in *choice*. The right choice brings about redemption because the wrong choice will leave the character in a worse moral condition.

The right choice saves the Lead from a damaged life (the life lived under the power of the negative side of his inner struggle).

In *Casablanca*, Rick, at the beginning, does not care what happens to other people. "I stick my neck out for nobody," he says. We see the inner struggle reflected on his face when the police arrest Ugarte at Rick's cafe. Ugarte begs for his life, but Rick, cheek muscles twitching, refuses.

At the end, he's given two choices. He can take another man's wife (who happens to be his true love, and who happens to look exactly like Ingrid Bergman), or he can sacrifice his greatest desire, even if it costs him his own life, for an even greater good.

We all know what happens.

If Rick had taken Ilsa, he would have remained damaged goods. Inevitably he'd continue drinking and knock Ilsa around.

Now, instead, because of choosing rightly, he goes off to become a true patriot.

To give your story added depth, envision the redemptive element. Is it offered to the Lead or to another character?

What choice is made, and what are the consequences?

A premise must be supported by fresh, solid scenes.

Scenes are the building blocks of fiction. A great premise will not stand without solid scenes to prop it up. Colorful characters can flit across the page, but unless they are engaged in pitched battle, the reader won't care.

Don't let your scenes fall into cliché or monotony. Always look for ways to freshen them up. Here are five techniques to help you do that.

1. MAKE YOUR DIALOGUE FLOW.

Try writing a scene only in dialogue. Let it flow. Don't think much about it. When you're finished, you can look back and figure out what the scene is really about.

I once wrote a scene between competing lawyers. Part of it went like this:

> "You think you can get away with that?"
>
> "Whatever works."
>
> "Disbarment works, too."
>
> "You want to try to prove that? Know what that'll make you look like?"

"Don't presume to know what I will or will
not do."

"I know you better than your wife, Phil."

That last line of dialogue came out of nowhere. Why
did the character say that? I could edit it out, of course, but
it seemed far better to explore the implications. What that
led to was a plot point where the one lawyer reveals he's had
an investigator on Phil for six months. And has pictures and
places and dates Phil will not want revealed to his wife.

All that just from playing with dialogue. Try it, and
you'll discover undercurrents for your scene you didn't
know were there.

2. CUT OR HIDE EXPOSITION.

Any time the author gives information in narrative
form, the immediate story is put on hold. This exposition, if you don't watch it, can bloat and choke off a
good scene.

The first thing to look for is exposition you don't
need. If it's not crucial for the moment, delay it. If it's not
crucial for the overall story, cut it. The more important
information can often be "hidden" by putting it into either dialogue or a character's thoughts.

Here's an example of clunky exposition:

Cosmo was a successful doctor, but he had
a dark secret. Early in his career he took out a

patient's liver, thinking it was an appendix. This caused him to turn heavily to drink, but he never let his colleagues or patients catch him at it. For all anyone knew, he was a pillar of the community.

Pretty dull. But what if Cosmo is sitting at his desk when his ex-wife bursts in holding a court order for more spousal support?

Cosmo looked up from his medical reports. "Mildred!"

"Court order," Millie said, throwing an ominous looking document in front of him.

"You can't just barge in like this! I have patients to see."

Millie laughed. "Don't play honorable doctor with me. I'm the one who had to pick you up at the local bars all those years. Still hiding the whiskey in your cotton jar?"

Cosmo cast a quick glance at the jar by the window, then turned back to his former spouse. "So what, are you going to try to smear me now?"

"If I wanted to smear you, I would have told the papers a long time ago about Mr. Santini and the young doctor who took out his liver."

"You're still holding that over my head?"

"How could anyone, let alone a doctor on the staff of a major hospital, mistake a liver for an appendix?" Millie shook her head.

"I'd like to mistake you for a cadaver!" Cosmo said. "I will not have my good name in this community besmirched by you!"

"See you in court." Millie turned and walked out of the room. Cosmo took a deep breath, then went to the cotton jar, opened it, and pulled out a bottle of Jack.

You get the idea. When in doubt, have two characters argue about something, and put some exposition in the argument. It works every time. Elmore Leonard once said, "All the information you need in a book can be put in dialogue."

Thoughts are another way to do this. Here's one from Millie's POV:

> Millie shook her head. He was so pathetic. Probably still on the juice, still trying to drown out the fact that he took out a liver during an appendectomy.

3. FLIP THE OBVIOUS.

Our minds work by reaching for the most familiar choices available. For writers, that usually means a cliché. So learn to flip things.

If your characters are mere types, your scenes won't engage the readers.

Imagine a truck driver rumbling down the highway at midnight, holding the steering wheel in one hand and a cup of hot, black coffee in the other.

Got that?

Now, I'll bet the first image your mind provided was of a burly male, probably wearing a baseball cap or cowboy hat. That's a familiar image of a trucker. It's a cliché, and therefore not very interesting.

But what if you flipped it around? What if the trucker was a woman?

Try it.

Now you have an image to play with. But I'll wager you still pictured a rather "tough" woman, because all truckers are tough, right?

Flip *that* around. Put this woman in a nice evening dress. What does that do for your image? Why is she dressed that way? Where is she going? Who is after her?

You can play this game with descriptions and even dialogue. For instance:

> "It's about time we started the meeting," Johnson said. "Let's do an agenda check."
>
> "Right," Smith said. "First item is the Norwood project. Second, the P&L statement. Third, employee benefits."

Stop a moment and flip the obvious response:

"It's about time we started the meeting," Johnson said. "Let's do an agenda check."

"Do it yourself," Smith said.

Or:

"Who picks your ties?"

"I quit."

"Jerk."

The nice part about this exercise is that even if you decide to stick with your original dialogue, the list you came up with provides you with possible subtext or insights about your character.

Play this game as long as you like, and you're guaranteed to come up with fresh material for characters, scenes, and dialogue.

4. APPLY THE CLOSED-EYES TECHNIQUE.

Describing a physical setting in rich detail is crucial to a vivid scene. Where do such details come from?

Say your hero has just entered a house where a friend lives. Close your eyes and "see" this house. Then record what you see as if you were a reporter on the scene. Describe all of the details as they are revealed to you. Later, go back and edit out what you don't need. But by doing it this way, you'll give yourself plenty of good, raw material to work with.

5. KNOW WHAT YOU'RE AIMING AT.

Every scene in your novel should have that moment or exchange that is the focal point, the bull's-eye, the thing you're aiming at. If your scene doesn't have a bull's-eye, it should be cut or rewritten.

A bull's-eye can be a few lines of dialogue that turn the action around or reveal something striking.

It can be as subtle as a moment of realization, or as explicit as a gunshot to the heart.

Many times, it is found in the last paragraph or two.

Identify that moment so you know what you're writing *toward*.

Then hit the bull's-eye. You may be a little off target in the first draft, but that's what rewriting is for. You'll hit it the second or third time.

34

When you are stuck, call on a word and its cousins.

As Sun Tzu said, the conditions of war are like water flowing over the ground. No constancy of form, so you have to be able to adapt.

Writing is like that. And that's a good thing. The flow keeps you from becoming formulaic. You need to train yourself to look for the new and the fresh at every critical stage of your writing.

Sometimes you'll get stuck. When that happens, I use a pocket thesaurus.

Say I'm writing about my character's background. I need to know what her father did for a living. I pull out my thesaurus, open to a page at random, and take the first word my eyes fall upon. I read that word and all the synonyms. Invariably, I get a web of pictures and possibilities for whatever I'm looking for, in this case a profession for the father.

For example, I just opened to the word *fugitive*. I see the definition, one who flees confinement, captivity, or justice, and synonyms like *escapee*, *refugee*, *runaway*. How about if my lead character's father is a bounty hunter? Or a prison guard? Or maybe even a real fugitive living under an assumed name? Or running away from a past

战 **114** 争

that may have included incarceration? All possibilities I can sift through, and I can keep going, making the list longer, which is always a good thing.

Or, let's say I have a scene where my character is reflecting on the events swirling around her, and I need some sort of action to take place to keep the scene from being overly introspective. I open to the word *peanuts*. There is a slang entry that says, "a small or trifling amount of money, as in he sold his car for peanuts." And the synonym *chicken food*.

Maybe my character is outside a park carnival and a guy tries to sell her some peanuts (or a chicken!) and won't go away. Why won't he go away? Why is he selling chickens out here? Maybe he becomes an intriguing secondary character.

Or maybe she's thinking about the need to get some money, and she wants to sell her car, but it's only worth peanuts. Why is her car only worth peanuts? Why didn't she have a better car? What does this tell me about her life?

And so on as far as I want to go. I will even use this technique when I'm in the middle of writing a scene and I need the dialogue to take an unexpected turn.

Whenever you find yourself with a little bit of writer's stuckness, whip out your thesaurus and look up a word. Let whatever happens in your mind happen. You will find a way to relate it to your story.

35

The use of a voice journal will keep characters from becoming little versions of the writer.

The voice journal is my favorite way of getting to know a character. The voice journal is simply a character speaking in stream-of-consciousness mode. You prompt the character by asking the occasional question, and then just let your fingers record the words on the page.

It's essential that you do not edit as you write. It's best to write in five- or ten-minute chunks, without stopping. Over and over again.

Here is what a voice journal might look like with a character I'm making up right now:

> My name is Pierpont Feenie, and people stare at me because I'm six foot nine. So what? That's the body I got, and that's the body I use. I go down to Venice Beach, and I play basketball. That's my thing. When I play basketball, I feel alive. I can jump, I can fly, I am the best there is on the black-top. They got guys down there, college guys who think they can bang with me, but I've got the sky

> hook, I've got the beef, and I love to lay them out.
> Laying them out keeps me from killing people. See,
> I used to be an assassin. The tallest assassin in
> the world.

When I started the voice journal, I did not know that Pierpont was an assassin. But he told me he was. So I wrote it down.

However, if this does not fit the needs of my story, it's very easy to change that and go on with something else.

Next, you can concentrate on background:

> I was born in New Jersey and grew up in the
> rough part of Newark. My dad died in a subway
> tunnel. Somebody pushed him off the platform.
> They never found out who. I was eight years old,
> and my mom didn't do too well after that. I had
> to take care of my little sisters. Twins. Two years
> younger than me. I had to grow up fast. The night
> our building caught on fire, well, that made me
> grow up even faster ...

Keep going with this. You will find yourself excited about your characters. You'll think about them even when you're not writing.

They will become real to you.

It's freaky. It's fun. And it makes for better characters in better stories.

Dwight Swain said that "zest" for your fiction is sustained primarily by creating unique characters. "Take it upon yourself to find something fresh and new in each and every [character]," Swain writes in *Creating Characters: How to Build Story People*. "Believe me, the process will excite you. And out of that excitement will come production."

The voice journal is the fastest way to that excitement.

Speed is the essence of the opening.

Sun Tzu wrote: "Speed is the essence of war: take advantage of the enemy's unreadiness, make your way by unexpected routes, and attack unguarded spots."

Steven Wright wrote: "My house is on the median strip of a highway. You don't really notice, except I have to leave the driveway doing sixty miles an hour."

This collective wisdom applies to the opening of your novel, for you are in a battle for attention. You must use all haste to surprise and capture the reader.

And I mean take him by the lapels and drag him into the story world with no time wasted.

Because everyone, with the possible exception of your mother (if she reads your work), has a little voice in his head ready to shout, "Life's too short. I don't have time to go on with this."

You must do all you can to attack and mute that voice, which is as anxious to spring as a mongoose outside the snake exhibit.

So how do you do it?

By understanding why people read.

They read to *worry*.

They read because they want to have their emotions wrenched by the plight of a character to whom they feel emotionally connected.

You do the connecting. You start connecting from paragraph one.

If you want to sell your fiction, you must *grab* the emotions of the reader by putting a character in some kind of discomfort or danger or the possibility thereof.

Immediately.

Big danger, little danger. Big challenge, little challenge. Anything that is a disturbance, or potential disturbance, to their ordinary world.

Because we naturally side with people who are in some sort of trouble.

Do you remember the opening shot of *The Wizard of Oz*? When I ask this question in writing classes, I usually get an immediate response that it's a shot of Miss Gulch on her bicycle. Or the barnyard in Kansas.

Actually, the first shot is Dorothy and Toto running down the road toward the farm. Dorothy is looking over her shoulder, and we find out later that Miss Gulch has threatened to take Toto in to be destroyed.

There is an immediate disturbance in Dorothy's ordinary world.

In chapter one of Stephenie Meyer's *Twilight*, teenage Bella moves to a small town and is immediately thrust into a new school. This is always disturbing. No friends, no history. We naturally identify.

The first line is:

> My mother drove me to the airport with the
> windows rolled down.

By the end of the paragraph, we know this is a fare-well. That's change. That's disturbance.

You can also *allude* to danger yet to come, as Dean Koontz does in *Fear Nothing*:

> On the desk in my candlelit study, the telephone
> rang, and I knew that a terrible change was coming.

Or to a disturbance that's already happened, and will be explained, as in Lawrence Block's *Ariel*:

> Was there a noise that woke her? Roberta was
> never sure.

A few more examples:

> I feel compelled to report that at the moment
> of death, my entire life did not pass before my
> eyes in a flash.
> —*"I" Is for Innocent* by Sue Grafton

> When the sixth floor of the Las Palmas Ho-
> tel caught fire Robbie Brownlaw was in the diner
> across the street about to have lunch.
> —*The Fallen* by T. Jefferson Parker

> The first time my husband hit me I was nineteen years old.
>
> —*Black and Blue* by Anna Quindlen

> "Do your neighbors burn one another alive?" was how Fraa Orolo began his conversation with Artisan Flec.
>
> —*Anathem*, by Neal Stephenson

You can also place the disturbance at the end of your first paragraph. Here is the opening of *The Day After Tomorrow* by Allan Folsom:

> Paul Osborn sat alone among the smoky bustle of the after-work crowd, staring into a glass of red wine. He was tired and hurt and confused. For no particular reason he looked up. When he did, his breath left him with a jolt. Across the room sat the man who murdered his father.

Harlan Coben does the delayed disturbance in *Promise Me*:

> The missing girl—there had been unceasing news reports, always flashing to that achingly ordinary school portrait of the vanished teen, you know the one, with the rainbow-swirl background, the girl's hair too straight, her smile too self-conscious, then a quick cut to the worried parents on the front

lawn, microphones surrounding them, Mom silent-
ly tearful, Dad reading a statement with quivering
lip—that girl, that *missing* girl, had just walked past
Edna Skylar.

The first line is intriguing (a good thing) but isn't
connected to a character until the last line. So there's a
hook, a build, and then *boom*.

Remember, speed in the opening is a matter of disturbance, not high levels of action. And it is applicable
to both literary and commercial fiction. The faster we
worry about a character, the quicker the bond. And the
greater our desire to turn the page.

Discipline clichéd or predictable story beginnings.

Here's how *not* to open your novel ...

WEATHER

You'll often hear from industry pros that they don't want to see books that begin with weather. They mean long descriptive passages up front.

You can indicate something about the weather, but only if you connect it to a viewpoint character and use it to add to the tone of the scene. Not this:

> The wind was chilly that January morning. Fluffy clouds dotted the sky as the sun's rays illuminated the trees. To the north, the threat of rain teased the mountains, which stood majestic in their winter garb.

Instead:

> Dalton heard the door slam and knew his wife had left. He didn't bother throwing on his robe. He ran downstairs in his boxers, and out the front door to head her off.

An arctic breeze assaulted him on the porch. He squinted in the morning light, obscured only a little by the clouds, and saw his wife backing out the car.

Dalton ran across the frosty grass in his bare feet and slipped.

DREAMS

Dreams in fiction are best left to the middle part of the story, to indicate strong emotion.

Making the first scene a dream is a kind of cheat. It gets the reader caught up in a situation that is full of portent, and then yanks that away with the "and then I woke up" routine. It's not much better when the writer lets you know it's a dream from the start. (With apologies to Daphne du Maurier and *Rebecca*).

Editors tend to view dream openings with suspicion. I know some wildly successful writers have opened novels with a dream. After you sell eight gazillion copies, you can do it too.

"HAPPY PEOPLE IN HAPPY LAND"

This is my term for the opening chapter that feels like pure setup. You have the nice family unit, all getting ready for the day, kissing each other and having breakfast, and then the husband goes off to work. At the end of chapter one, or the beginning of chapter two, the wife gets the report that the husband has died in a car accident.

Not soon enough.

So what can you do if you absolutely insist on having a "normal life" opening chapter, after you've considered every other alternative?

You can at least put in a portent at the beginning, enough to carry the reader along for a few pages.

Dean Koontz opens *Tick Tock* like this:

> Out of a cloudless sky on a windless November day came a sudden shadow that swooped across the bright aqua Corvette. Tommy Phan was standing beside the car, in pleasantly warm autumn sunshine, holding out his hand to accept the keys from Jim Shine, the salesman, when the fleeting shade touched him. He heard a brief thrumming like frantic wings. Glancing up, he expected to glimpse a sea gull, but not a single bird was in sight.

The scene continues as Tommy Phan gets the keys to the Corvette (which inexplicably chill him) and happily drives away, talks to his mother on the phone, and so on with his normal life. But the portentous opening images and feelings give us a little breath of disturbance to carry us along.

Learn to pace your scene openings for specific effects.

Take a look at these two scene openings:

Opening #1

We drove back to the cabin. I found the key under the mat, as promised, and unlocked the door.

A musty smell hit me as I opened the door and motioned Sarah to go in. Fortunately, the electricity was on and I found the light switch.

I asked Sarah to sit on the couch, and she did. "Now," I said, "what is this thing that couldn't wait?"

"I'm pregnant," she said.

Opening #2

"I'm pregnant," Sarah said.

"You're what?"

She was sitting on the couch in the cabin, which, fortunately, I'd been able to get into. It was cold and musty, but I didn't notice any of it. Not now.

Number two gives us the action first, *then* the setting information.

If you want to create page-turning momentum, open more of your scenes this way.

To slow things down for pacing, open more like the first way.

Just don't wait *too long* to let the reader know why the scene is here, and why it is important.

39

Remember that love means never having to say, "I love you."

Don't let your characters say "I love you" to anyone, especially those they love.

Saying "I love you" is manipulative and a cliché.

It's a plea for sympathy.

It's flat.

Instead, *show* your characters loving. Adding the words (or relying on them) actually dilutes the emotional content you're going for.

An exception may be made if your character is pleading, arguing, wondering, or otherwise has some point to make other than the plain, one-to-one sentiment of *I + love + you*.

But still see if you can do it any other way.

If you can't, fine. Put it in. But make it a fight before you do.

And if it's going to be in there, freshen it up, as in this beat from Woody Allen's *Annie Hall*:

> ANNIE: Do you love me?
>
> ALVY: I-uh, love is, uh, is too weak a word for what ...

ANNIE: Yeah.

ALVY: —I ... I *lerve* you. You know, I *loove* you, I *loff* you. There are two *f*'s. I have to invent a word, ... Of course I love you.

Characters all alone should do more than think.

You may want to have a character alone in a scene, thoughts rattling around in his head. You do this to show a bit of the inside, the emotions going on. Fine.

But the longer the beat goes on, the more you need to get some action in there as counterpoint. Too much introspection all at once gets wearying.

In James Grippando's *Last Call*, jail escapee Isaac Reems is hiding out in a vacant house up for sale. Now he has to assess his next move and his need for a change of clothes—the one's he has on he stole from a homeless guy.

So Reems has a plot problem: Where to go next?

He thinks about it.

But to keep this from being just a thinking scene, Grippando throws Reems another little challenge: bugs. The clothes he stole are infested, so now he's got them all over his skin and hair.

He tears off the clothes and jumps in the shower. Now he's really up the creek in the clothes department.

But Grippando doesn't stop there. An old man is walking his poodle past the house. The poodle sees Reems.

The miniature white poodle was barking and bouncing up and down like a Ping-Pong ball, as if to shout, "Run for your life—there's a black man in the house!"

So Reems has yet another problem, and looks for a solution to this barking dog. He picks up a hammer.

End of scene. Well done. *Because we want to find out what happens to the poor poodle!* But Grippando, skilled suspense writer that he is, makes us wait.

And that's how you write a scene that's not just *thinking*.

Apply the Spencer Tracy secret for creating memorable characters.

Sun Tzu wrote: "All warfare is based on deception."

So is fiction. As Lawrence Block put it, it's telling lies for fun and profit.

Acting is based on deception, too, which brings me to Spencer Tracy.

Tracy was considered the best among his peers. Bogart said you could never see the "gears turning" in Tracy. He was completely natural, and it didn't matter if he was doing comedy or drama.

So what was his big secret? What was his technique? As Tracy explained in an interview, "I've finally narrowed it down to where, when I begin a part, I say to myself, this is Spencer Tracy as a judge, or this is Spencer Tracy as a priest or as a lawyer, and let it go at that. Look, the only thing an actor has to offer a director and finally an audience is his instinct. That's all."

This is the way to come up with living, breathing characters in your writing, too.

I don't know about you, but I've never been able to fill out one of those long dossier forms for my characters.

I like to have certain essential information, of course: vocation, looks, general personality type, a bit of background. But from there, I want to hear and see the character, which is why I choose a visual (there are many sources of images on the Web) and use the voice journal.

The Spencer Tracy secret is another way of getting into your characters, viscerally. Think about being *you as the character*.

This may remind you of the famous "method school" of acting, popularized by Marlon Brando. The method is just a way of getting at the same thing. How can actors *become* the characters they play so as to achieve emotional immediacy?

There's been a lot of ink spilled on the method, but I think it is best summed up by what the Russian director Constantin Stanislavski called the "Magic If." It simply means to act *as if* you were that character. In all rehearsals, that's what you go for, until you begin to feel the part.

So if you are loathe to approach those long questionnaires about your characters, the Spencer Tracy secret may be for you.

Robert Gregory Browne says:

> If my lead character is a divorced father of three who finds himself unwittingly involved in a conspiracy to overthrow the government, the first thing I ask myself when approaching a scene (even though I'm

happily married and wouldn't know a conspiracy if it jumped up and bit me) is this: How would I react in this situation.

Then I add the color (read: attitude/emotion). How would I react if ... I was a no-nonsense cop ... an officious political hack. And I apply this technique to every character I write.

In short, I'm like a method actor playing all of the parts. By using myself and a healthy dose of imagination, I can approach characterization from the inside out. And once I'm able to get into the skin of my characters, it's much, much easier to create someone whom I, and hopefully the audience, can identify with.

Utilize the Q Factor as a strategic weapon for motivation at just the right time.

When I teach fiction writing at a conference, I usually spend a few minutes talking about something I call the Q Factor. It comes from the character in the James Bond movies, the one who is always giving Bond his gadgets and telling him not to play with them. There is a very important reason this character exists.

Let's cut ahead to the inevitable James Bond ending. Bond has been hung by his ankles over a school of piranha. The bad guy grins and says something like, "Enjoy your swim, Mr. Bond." Then he sets the timer to lower James Bond into the pool of piranha and, of course, leaves. (An interesting existential question is why villains so often leave before their adversaries are dispatched.)

As Bond is lowered toward his doom, he manages to get his thumb on one of his cufflinks. The cufflink turns into a small, rotating saw. He uses that saw to cut through the restraints on his hands.

Now he is able to reach into his jacket pocket and pull out a fountain pen. The fountain pen is, in reality, a device that holds a compressed nitrogen charge and

战**136**争

shoots a small grappling hook and line across the piranha pond, enabling Bond to cut his leg restraints and swing to safety on the other side of the pool.

Now, if we had been reading along in the story and gotten to this point, and Bond simply produced those items for the first time, we'd all be groaning. How convenient! What a cheat!

But of course, it was all set up by the Q scene. Because we saw these items before, we are perfectly accepting of them when they come out at the right time.

In fiction, the Lead character should reach a point near the end when everything looks lost. This can be something outside or inside the character, or both. But he is, in figurative terms, dangling over a pool of piranha.

What he needs is courage for the final battle, to face the ultimate test. This is where the Q Factor can help. It is something that is set up early in the story that will provide the necessary inspiration or instruction for the character when he needs it most.

Sometimes, the Q Factor is an icon of some sort, a physical object. Sometimes, it is the memory of a beloved mentor. It may simply be the character digging down into his moral reservoir. Whatever it may be, it is the storyteller's job to give it life on the page.

In the great Frank Capra film *Mr. Smith Goes to Washington*, the naïve young senator played by James Stewart arrives in Washington, D.C. for the first time. He is mesmerized by the city that represents everything he loves about America. So he slips away from his handlers and goes on a sightseeing tour, which is rendered in a wonderful montage. The montage ends at the Lincoln Memorial. Here, young Jefferson Smith is deeply moved by what he sees. He reads the words inscribed on the wall. He sees a young boy holding his grandfather's hand, trying to say the words aloud. He observes an African-American gentleman removing his hat. And then Smith looks back up at the face of Lincoln.

We now have a very emotional object embedded in our minds.

At the end of Act 2, Mr. Smith knows he is a political puppet of a corrupt machine and has no way of fighting back. He has even been betrayed by a senior senator who had been a good friend of his father's. Smith takes this as the final knife in his back and decides to leave town.

It's nighttime, and he is passing the Lincoln Memorial, but this time defeated and downcast. He sits heavily on the steps.

Along comes the political operative played by Jean Arthur. Originally, she thought of Smith as a dumb oaf, too, but she has come to respect his integrity in this sea of cynicism. She says, "I had a hunch I'd find you here ..." And then she says, "Remember the first day you got here? Remember what you said about Mr. Lincoln? You said he was sitting up there waiting for someone to come along. You were right. He was waiting for a man who could see his job and sail into it, that's what he was waiting for. A man who could tear into the Taylors and root 'em out into the open. I think he was waiting for you, Jeff. He knows you can do it. So do I."

Smith gets inspired, and as they walk away, he pauses to wave at Lincoln.

Now, when Mr. Smith undertakes the impossible task of a single-man filibuster, we understand and accept how he could do that. That's the Q Factor.

Another example: When Luke Skywalker is engaged in a final battle in *Star Wars*, he hears the voice of Obi-Wan telling him to remember to use the Force. Inspiration.

In a lot of old movies, you'll have the Lead character reaching the dark point, and hearing, in echoing tones, the voice of something his father or mother told him a long time ago. A moral sentiment that inspires the Lead once more.

Sometimes, the Q Factor can be a negative emotion. In *High Noon*, the classic Western starring Gary Cooper as Will Kane, Kane finds himself as one man against four killers. The townspeople have all come up with excuses not to help him. He knows he will probably die. And the real bummer is that he has just married Grace Kelly!

There comes a point just before the climax when Kane is considering getting a horse and riding out of town. He will get together with his wife again and go somewhere and try to live without being found. He's in a livery stable, considering this.

Enter the character of Harvey, played by Lloyd Bridges. Harvey is a coward and hates being in the shadow of the great Will Kane. He sees Kane and knows that if he can get him to ride out of town, in effect showing the town that Kane is really a coward after all, then he, Harvey, will look good in comparison.

As Harvey tries to get Kane to do this, Kane realizes that if he does go, he will be no better than Harvey. And that's when he makes the decision to stay. Harvey, who was introduced early in the film, is the negative Q Factor for Kane's decision.

Think of it this way. So many stories are about over-coming fear. The fear manifests itself most when all the forces are marshaled against the Lead. Fear and common sense tell her to give up, run away.

She knows she can't. So give her a Q Factor, an emotional element that comes in when she needs it. To do that:

1. Select what the element will be (item, mentor, moral sentiment, negative character).

2. Write a scene early in the narrative that anchors this element emotionally to the Lead.

3. Refer to the Q Factor once in the middle section, as a reminder. You should do this subtly, almost as a throwaway.

4. Find a trigger point in the Lead's darkest hour where the Q Factor can be reintroduced.

5. Show the Lead taking new action based on the Q Factor. If you've embedded the Q Factor well enough up front, the readers will pick up what's happening without you having to explain it to them. Just let it happen naturally.

Give backstory the proper respect, and it will help readers bond with your characters.

Poor backstory. It gets no respect these days.

I was in a crowded elevator at a writers' conference after teaching a class on great opening chapters (wherein I had been cheeky enough to use one of my own as an example). A bespectacled fellow complimented me, then added, "I did notice, though, that in the opening chapter of *your* novel, you had backstory. The rule is *no backstory*."

Almost everyone in the elevator nodded in silent agreement.

I'm always fascinated how "viral rules" get propagated among the writing masses. It's like the super flu in *The Stand*. Maybe it starts in a critique group, gets put up on a blog, and, pretty soon, it becomes accepted wisdom.

Not always for the best.

In fact, backstory has an important part to play in the opening of your novel. But it must be properly understood what that role is.

First, a definition. *Backstory* is what has happened before the present story begins, usually related to the Lead character's history. And there's the potential problem.

We want a story to begin now, in the present, with a *disturbance*. With *trouble*.

A disturbance *connected to the character*. That's the key to the proper use of backstory. *It should not be used to help set up the story.* Many new writers think the reader needs a bunch of backstory to understand who the character is and why she is in this opening scene. They don't. Readers will happily wait a long time for the background if you have a character dealing with a disturbance.

But using backstory judiciously is important *because it helps bond the reader with the character.* Backstory deepens that bond via *emotion* and *sympathy*.

When we know something of the character's life, how she got into this opening situation, and why the disturbance matters so much, we get invested in her.

And that's when your opening really starts to cook.

The main mistake new writers make is what I call *backdumping*, the piling up of backstory early on, even on the first page, deadening the effect of forward motion. Back when people had actual attention spans—the golden era of actual attention spans being 1774 to 1879—a novelist could take a long time up front laying out the history of a character.

Those days are over. You must begin with a character and *drop in backstory in little bits as the need arises*.

Some types of fiction can be a little more liberal with backstory. An epic, for example. Historical, science-fiction, and generational epics can start with more history because the readers expect it. The sheer size of the book signals that it's coming.

You want that kind of backstory? Read James Michener's *Hawaii*, which begins "Millions upon millions of years ago ..." Or *Alaska*, which begins "About a billion years ago ..."

Now that's when backstory had hair on its chest.

But unless you are writing such a book, use the *active drop* for *relevant* backstory in your opening chapters. That's the subject of the next section.

44

The dropping in of backstory should be active.

The *active drop* means you establish an active scene first—a character in motion, facing a disturbance—then you drop in backstory *within the action itself*.

In his novel *The House of Sand and Fog*, Andre Dubus III begins with action, with the character of Massoud Behrani narrating:

> The fat one, the radish Torez, he calls me camel because I am Persian and because I can bear this August sun longer than the Chinese and the Panamanians and even the little Vietnamese, Tran. He works very quickly without rest, but when Torez stops the orange highway truck in front of the crew, Tran hurries for his paper cup of water with the rest of them. The heat is no good for work. All morning we have walked this highway between Sausalito and the Golden Gate Park. We carry our small trash harpoons and we drag our burlap bags and we are dressed in vests the same color as the highway truck.

We have one bit of active drop: the narrator is Persian, but he does not simply describe himself that way. He does it because another character calls him a name.

The scene continues when a worker named Mendez gets in Behrani's face. Then:

> I pull my sack over my shoulder and to Mr. Torez I say: "In my country I could have ordered him beaten."
>
> "Sí, Camello? In Mendez's country he would have beaten you himself."
>
> "I was colonel, Mr. Torez. I was colonel in the Imperial Air Force. Do you know this, Mr. Torez? I was a *colonel*."

More backstory comes in, this time via dialogue. And since dialogue is action, you have an automatic active drop.

Behrani and the crew begin to eat lunch (action). Then the following:

> In my country, I was not only a desk officer; I bought F-16 jets from Israel and the United States, and when I was a captain in Tehran, a genob sarvan, I worked on the engines with my own hands. Of course, all the best aerocompanies are here in California but in four years I have spent hundreds of dollars copying my credentials; I have worn my French suits and my Italian shoes to hand-deliver

> my qualifications; I have waited and then called
> back after the correct waiting time; but there
> is nothing.

This is simple narration, but we accept it because we are within an active scene.

What we know now is that Massoud Behrani was in a position of great respect in his old country, has been searching for a job for years, but is reduced to picking up trash. We learn more as the chapter continues, with Dubus alternating between action and backstory.

David Morrell begins *Scavenger* this way:

> He no longer called her by his dead wife's
> name, even though the resemblance was strong
> enough to make his heart ache. Sometimes, when
> he woke and found her sitting next to his hospital
> bed, he thought he was hallucinating.
>
> "What's my name?" she asked.
>
> "Amanda," he was careful to answer.
>
> "Excellent," a doctor said. The watchful man
> never mentioned his specialty, but Balenger as-
> sumed he was a psychiatrist. "I think you're ready
> to be released."

The first two lines show us the disturbance. A man in a hospital bed. Backstory—his wife is dead—is mentioned within the action itself.

The scene continues with Amanda and Balenger in a taxi, driving through Brooklyn and then about to enter her apartment.

> Amanda put a key in the lock.
> "Wait," Balenger said.
> "Need to catch your breath?"
> In fact, he did, but that wasn't his motive for stopping her. "Are you sure this is a good idea?"
> "Do you have another place to go, anyone else to take care of you?"
> In both cases the answer was "no." During the previous year, while Balenger searched for his missing wife, he stayed in cheap motel rooms and could afford to eat only once a day, mostly sandwiches from fast-food restaurants. His savings account was drained. He had no one and nothing. [*backstory*]
> "You barely know me," he told her.
> "You risked your life for me," Amanda responded. "Without you, I'd be dead. [*backstory*] What else do I need to know?"
> Neither commented that at the time Balenger believed the woman he saved was his wife. [*backstory*]
> "We'll try it for a few days." Amanda unlocked the door.

Morrell has set up an intriguing opening, definitely a disturbance to the Lead's ordinary world, and used the active drop for a bit of backstory. My interest in the Lead has been elevated.

Go through your opening chapter and highlight every bit of backstory. Cut what can be delayed until later. Use only what is useful for establishing some sort of empathy with the character. Then drop those in *actively*.

Action first.

45

Progressive revelation keeps readers turning pages.

Reveal your plot incrementally. That means leaving mystery inherent and unfolding things progressively. That keeps readers reading.

Do not reveal everything about your Lead up front. Do drop in hints and actions that make the reader wonder, "Why is this happening?" or "Why is she doing that? Feeling that?"

Pull the reader along with unanswered questions, saving the final revelations until well into the book.

John Gilstrap does this masterfully in *At All Costs*. In chapter one, we see Jake Brighton, by all accounts a highly competent body shop manager for a Ford dealer. He's going about his business when a heavily-armed team of feds bust in and arrest him. As he's handcuffed and on the floor:

> He fought back the urge to sneeze and tried
> to make the pieces fit in his mind.
> We've been so careful.

Careful about what? Gilstrap doesn't tell us. Not until the final line of the chapter:

> He wondered if he and Carolyn still owned
> the top slots on the Ten Most Wanted list.

Whoa! But then another question is raised: What could this outwardly normal and hardworking man have done to be at the top of the FBI list?

Again, Gilstrap makes us wait. For almost a hundred pages. As Jake and his wife, Carolyn, try to escape town with their thirteen-year-old son, putting a long ago plan into effect, we are drawn further in by the mystery of their background. (In a nice twist, not even the son knows what his parents have done.)

It is only when the chase is on that Gilstrap reveals their hidden secret. By then we care for these people *and* we are hooked by the action, all because of progressive revelation.

Dialogue will compel the turning of pages if it is a compression and extension of action.

Bloated, clunky, dull dialogue is a five-alarm warning to the reviewer that you can't write salable fiction.

Crisp, crackling dialogue, differentiated among the characters (so they don't all sound the same) instills a feeling of confidence in the reviewer.

Everyone loves great dialogue.

So, how do you crank yours up?

By remembering the most important rule of all, a definition that comes from the noted playwright and screenwriter John Howard Lawson (also one of the blacklisted Hollywood Ten in the 1950s). Dialogue, he said, must be viewed as "a compression and extension of action."[1]

That means you never have a character say anything that is unconnected to that character's objective in a scene.

And every character in every scene must have an objective, otherwise he shouldn't be there. Replace him with a chair.

1 Lawson, John Howard, *Theory and Technique of Playwriting*, (NY, Putnam, 1936, P. 288.)

With this in mind, try the following:

1. Before you write a scene, review in your mind what each character wants *at that moment in time.*

2. Make sure the objectives come into conflict. It doesn't have to be *direct* conflict, though much of the time that is to be preferred. It can be as simple as one character being distracted so the other one can't get through. Or one character trying to avoid direct answers and hesitating all over the place. Anything but pure back-and-forth agreement.

3. Review your dialogue after it's written, asking, *How do these lines help my character realize her objective? How is she using the dialogue as an extension or compression of action?*

47

The innovative writer will sometimes write dialogue only, then fill in the blanks.

Scenes, as we previously discussed, are the building blocks of fiction. So the writer has to ask, *What's this scene going to be about?* And then he writes it.

That's the normal routine anyway. But how do you discover what the scene is about in the first place?

You can think it through first and then write. Or you can write some of it first and let it unfold.

The best way to do the latter is through dialogue.

Decide who is going to be in the scene. Give each person an agenda, and let them start talking. The dialogue you write will become the raw material for your scene. You can justify what comes out of their mouths later.

What happens when you do this is that a character will often say something you didn't expect. That's what you need to explore.

Stop and do some brainstorming. How does this new aspect of character fit into the story? Is it something you want to keep? If not, you can always backspace and have the character say something different.

Often, a line of dialogue will give you a new focus for the scene, a different motivation or agenda. Play with it.

48

For scenes to move with deliberate speed, the writer must grasp the truth behind RUE.

RUE stands for Resist the Urge to Explain. You'll find it in several writing books and all over Internet writing sites. For some, RUE means avoiding excess exposition. For others, it's another way of saying *show, don't tell*.

Both are valid observations.

When you can cut exposition, do it. Readers like mystery, and they will allow you to hide information so long as the action is moving along. Put off explanations for as long as possible. Only use what is absolutely essential to the understanding of the moment.

You all know about showing versus telling, so watch for all those little explanatory phrases that can so easily sneak into your scenes. This is best illustrated by example.

> I ran through the forest, my heart pounding. I could hear the bloodhounds behind me, and the lawmen shouting instructions.
>
> I dug deep for air and willed my feet to move. Then skidded to a stop.

> Two feet ahead of me was a cliff.
> This was terrible. Dogs behind me and a drop
> in front.
> Spinning around, I saw the glint of a gun in
> the woods.

The RUE lines are: "This was terrible. Dogs behind me and a drop in front." The first line tells the reader what *he already feels* because of the action.

The second line repeats information already given. Without those lines, the scene would read:

> I ran through the forest, my heart pounding.
> I could hear the bloodhounds behind me, and the
> lawmen shouting instructions.
> I dug deep for air and willed my feet to move.
> Then skidded to a stop.
> Two feet ahead of me was a cliff.
> Spinning around, I saw the glint of a gun in
> the woods.

Much better. The tension does not abate, and the reader is experiencing the action along with the narrator.

The clever use of narrative dialogue will avoid the sin of small talk.

Here's a technique that will do two things: a) eliminate plain vanilla dialogue sections, and b) give you a chance to characterize. I call this *narrative dialogue*.

The term is a riff on *narrative summary*, which is what you do when you want to transition from one scene to the next, or cover some expanse of time without going step by step (and ending up with a 2,000-page novel).

Simply put, you use limited amounts of narrative to cover ground that doesn't contain essential conflict. If it does contain essential conflict, you should show us the scene, beat by beat.

Narrative summary is like this.

> They got in the car and sped toward L.A. Two
> hours later they pulled into the parking lot across
> from Pershing Square.

So, too, with narrative dialogue. Instead of giving us the actual talk, you summarize it through the POV character. Why would you do this? Primarily to eliminate dialogue that does not contain tension but does help us understand the characters.

Here is a section from one of John D. MacDonald's Travis McGee novels, *The Girl in the Plain Brown Wrapper*. McGee has just met a woman named Penny in a bar and they go through introductions and small talk. Too much of that in actual dialogue form would be boring. MacDonald gives us summary:

> So Trav was in town to see a man interested in putting some money in a little company called Floatation Associates, and Penny was a receptionist-bookkeeper in a doctor's office. Trav wasn't married, and Penny had been, four years ago, for a year, and it didn't take. And it sure had been a rainy summer and fall. Too much humidity. And the big thing about Simon and Garfunkel was the words to the songs, *reely*. If you read the lyrics right along with the songs while the record was on, you know, the lyrics right on the record case, it could really turn you on, like that thing about Silence especially. Don't you think, honest now, that when people like the same things and have enjoyed the same things, like before they ever met, Trav, it is sort of as if they had known each other a long time, instead of just meeting? And people don't have enough chance to just talk. People don't

communicate anymore somehow, and so everybody goes around kind of lonesome and out of
touch, sort of.

We catch the sense of the woman and of McGee's attitude here, in short order, so the story can go on.

50

Success may be found in three great scenes, and no weak ones.

The legendary film director John Huston (*The Maltese Falcon*, *The Treasure of the Sierra Madre*, *The African Queen*) once remarked that the secret to a successful film was three great scenes, and no weak ones.

Great scenes make memorable fiction, too. Scenes where the combatants are operating to the full. Passions run high; stakes run higher. What happens in the scene affects the rest of the story, and in a big way.

Weak scenes don't have this juice. They feel like fluff or filler. No one is really going after anything. There's a lot of sitting around, small talk, waiting, reacting.

In your novel planning, think about potential big scenes. Jot some notes about them, think about where they might land in your structure. A climactic scene near the end is a good place to start. If you can come up with something memorable right away, it's a scene to write toward. That'll give you a through line to guide your plotting.

When the first draft is done, look for weak scenes. Always be asking this question: *Is there any place in my manuscript where a tired, overworked editor can feel tempted to put the manuscript down?*

Cut that scene or make it matter. And keep cutting until there are no more weak scenes.

Next, find three scenes to elevate into greatness. This doesn't mean the rest of your book will have mediocre scenes. No! Every scene must work on its own, adding to the whole. Every scene needs tension and a strong readability quotient.

But three scenes should be elevated relative to the rest. These scenes need to be packed with conflict, emotion, and surprise.

All three.

Conflict. Emotion. Surprise.

Conflict is the engine of fiction, of course. Crank up the conflict. How?

Through *emotion*. Make sure the readers see the stakes to the inner life of the character.

Finally, give us something *surprising*—the unexpected setback, revelation, or question raised by the events.

Let's take John Huston's screenplay of *The Maltese Falcon*. The script has no weak scenes. (I might add, credit goes to Dashiell Hammett's novel as well, as the script is very faithful to the book.) And for me, at least three stand out.

Sam Spade's first meeting with the Fat Man, Gutman, is one of them. Spade has gone to Gutman to find out about this black bird everyone's interested in. In addition to the conflict and simmering emotions, there are two surprises I like.

First is Gutman himself. He is (especially as portrayed by Sydney Greenstreet) a unique antagonist—enormous, well dressed, speaking odd little bromides: "I distrust a closed-mouth man. He generally picks the wrong time to talk and says the wrong things."

Then, at the end of the scene, Spade pulls a bluff by pretending to lose his temper. The sudden switch catches both Gutman and the audience by surprise. When Spade slams the door and walks out, a little smile creeps across his face.

Two other scenes to mention.

One takes place in Spade's apartment with Brigid O'Shaughnessy (Mary Astor) and Cairo (Peter Lorre) present, and the cops arrive at the front door. Spade won't let them in. Cairo screams and the police rush in. Brigid has attacked Cairo. Then, with the police present, she kicks Cairo. It's a surprise, because it's so unlike her to lose her cool and act like a school girl.

The other great scene is the last one, where Spade tells Brigid that she's going to take the fall. The emotion is evident in Spade, because he has, in spite of himself, fallen for her. But he also knows how bad she is. He won't play the sap for her. He lets her be led off by the cops.

Which gives us a final tip: One of your three big scenes should be at or very near the end.

Give us three scenes like this in your novel and no weak ones. That's the secret.

51

To write comedy, make the characters believe they are in a tragedy.

A good comedy works when the characters *in* the comedy think they're in a *tragedy*, but the audience knows they are not.

It's really only *trivial tragedy* because the characters have blown something so out of proportion it becomes a matter of "life and death" for them.

Every *Seinfeld* episode is like that. Jerry, for example, sometimes has to choose between some silly thing and a great girlfriend. Like in the Soup Nazi episode. When the choice comes, he chooses the soup.

Or when Kramer and Newman come up with an elaborate scheme for making extra pennies on discarded bottles, planning every bit of it as if they were taking out Fort Knox.

Or when George wants to be able to nap under his desk at Yankee Stadium. Why? Because avoiding hard work is essential to his happiness.

For Oscar Madison in *The Odd Couple*, being a slob is essential to *his* happiness. When Felix threatens that with his neat-freakiness, Oscar thinks the situation is a Wagnerian catastrophe.

For Michael Dorsey in *Tootsie*, being an actor is all he knows, but no one will hire him. So he becomes Dorothy Michaels to get a part. We understand that because getting a part is all he is about, until he becomes a better man.

Trivial tragedy is the foundation of comedy writing. Set that up as a foundation, then make things go wrong so the characters don't get what they want.

52

To the question of whether to outline or not to outline: Yes.

So how do you write a *New York Times* bestseller?

You do an outline.

Or not.

Simple, isn't it?

Andrew Gross has been called the "high priest of outliners," and will do outlines of up to eighty pages before he begins writing. Gross, *New York Times* best-selling author of *The Blue Zone* and *The Dark Tide*, learned his outlining craft from James Patterson. His outlines keep him from writer's block. "I always know what I need to write on any given day," he says.

He advises writers just starting out to learn the discipline. "I want to control the plot," he says. "I don't want the plot controlling me."

On the other hand, Lee Child asserts, "I don't even know what I'm going to write in the next paragraph."

Two approaches. Two successes.

So who's right?

Both.

Some writers, perhaps most, are NOPs—No Outline People. They prefer the creative freedom to frolic across the land, to and fro, smelling the flowers, writing whatever pleases you.

Others will admit to being OPs, Outline People, though how extensively they do it is an open question. Some are minimalists with outlines, others like the extended version.

Some are authors who fall in between, like best-selling author Michael Palmer. "I have had to shorten my outlines in terms of how much of each chapter I write and also in terms of how far into the book I outline," Palmer says. "I haven't found that elusive balance between how much to outline before I start writing, and how much writing to get done before moving ahead with more outline. Sure wish I had unlimited time and unlimited money. Then I could write a really boffo outline before I start to write."

Carla Neggers puts it this way. "When someone asks me if I'm an outliner or a seat-of-the-pants writer, I say *yes*. I don't have a set technique. It depends on the book. A synopsis is a jumping off point for me. I do best when I focus on what I call the forward momentum of the story versus forcing myself to write a certain way. If forward momentum means stopping and outlining, I stop and outline. If it means going back to page one and rewriting, I go back to page one and rewrite. If it means writing in a whoosh without pausing to revise ... that's what I do. I'm disciplined as a writer but not regimented."

An outline is simply the organizing of your imagination. You have to do that at some point. NOPs usually do it at the end of a draft. OPs do it first.

NOPs usually have more heavy rewriting and editing to do with their drafts, but like the spontaneity. OPs put that time in up front, and are spontaneous with their outlining. They will tell you, too, that it's easier to change an outline than a full novel.

I always outline my first act extensively, then keep track of "signpost scenes," scenes I know I need to have at some point. In the early days, I used index cards, a product of my screenwriting training. There are now software programs that do pretty much the same thing.

The only advice I can give here is that you try things out. If you've never liked outlining, why not invest a couple of weeks and try to whip one up? Even if it drives you batty, you'll learn a lot about the story bubbling inside you.

And you outliners, if during the writing a character refuses to obey you, let him have a few minutes to explain himself. Be prepared to tweak your outline as needed.

Any novel, if it is to live, has to be able to breathe a little. "Slowly, slowly, I am learning to listen to the book, in the same way I try to listen in prayer," Madeleine L'Engle once wrote. "If the book tells me to do something completely unexpected, I heed it; the book is usually right."

53

The writer who is anxious to start writing should follow a mini-plan.

As soon as an idea starts to jell in my head, I want to start writing. I'm impatient. I've got a lot of ideas at various stages, and sometimes I just want to *go*, Kerouac style.

So I've developed a mini plan of action that lets me write some, and also gets to the next stage of my preplanning. If you're one of the impatient ones, maybe these steps will work for you.

1. Write a logline—that's a one-line concept-summary of your idea. Work this until it juices you. Don't settle for plain vanilla.

   > An insurance salesman and a hot, upper crust woman plot to murder her husband, for double the insurance payout.

2. Expand the logline into "back cover" copy.

   > Slick insurance man Walter Neff thinks he's got the world on a string. And then he meets Phyllis Dietrichson, the hot young wife of one of his clients. Maybe it's that

anklet she wears. Or maybe it's the smell of honeysuckle in the air.

Whatever it is, it's murder.

Driven by lust and greed, Walter helps Phyllis plan the murder of her husband. Walter knows how to make it look like an accident so Phyllis can collect under the double indemnity clause.

There's one problem, and his name is Barton Keyes. A legendary insurance investigator, he can sniff out a fraud from miles away. Walter knows everything has to be perfect. And so it seems.

Until that night on the train ...

Your cover copy doesn't have to be perfect. But it does have to excite you enough to keep going.

3. Write the opening disturbance. You know enough about your characters to do this. Get a visual in your mind. Cast the characters. You can use any actor, living or dead. For Walter, you might imagine, oh, say, Fred MacMurray. Or Mickey Rooney. For Phyllis, maybe you'll think of Barbara Stanwyck or Kate Winslet.

Now write an opening chapter according to the guidelines in "Speed is the essence of the opening." on page 119.

4. Write the next scene. Make more trouble, or give the reaction of the characters to what just happened.

5. Brainstorm. First, make a list of twenty things that could happen next. Fast. Don't think too much.

   Next, brainstorm about your Lead character. Deepen her. Give her inner struggles and conflicts. Do a voice journal for her.

   Plan three more scenes.

6. Write those scenes.

Now take a week just to play with what you've done, rewrite things, try a different POV, outline. Play.

   Your novel will be growing naturally. And you've hardly broken a sweat.

54

The wise writer draws on select weapons to keep his story moving forward.

So you're writing along and you get stuck. You don't know where to take the story or scene next. Maybe things are just dragging. What do you do? One of these:

1. Turn to a random page in a dictionary or thesaurus and select a word. Make a list of twenty things that occur to you from that word. (See "When you are stuck, call on a word and its cousins." on page 114).

2. Stop where you are, put in a marker of some kind in your document (I use ***) so you can find your way back, and skip ahead and write another scene.

3. When you get to the end of a scene and don't know where to go next, make two lists of at least ten items each:

   a. The first list is all the things you can think of that readers would *expect* to happen next.

b. The second list is all the things that could happen that are *not* what readers would expect. Write your new scenes based on the second list.

4. Stop and do some research. Talk to an expert. Read a book. Google some articles. Find a new and interesting nugget and work it into the story.

5. Switch the point of view. Rewrite the scene in first person if you're in third, or vice versa, and see what happens.

6. Go backward to the point in the story where things got slow or predictable and create a new path.

7. Start a new voice journal for the point-of-view character and ask her some questions about what's going on. Let the character tell you what's happening and why things are stalling. Then have the character come up with a solution.

8. Bring a new character into the scene. Make it a startling entrance and figure out how to justify it later.

9. Open a novel at random and flip pages until you find dialogue. Take the first line of dialogue you see and put it into the mouth of your point-of-view character and start writing a scene from there. Why did she just say that?

10. If things get really bad, eat a Ding Dong and lie down for half an hour. (You are allowed to substitute for the Ding Dong.) When you get up, write in longhand for five minutes straight, without stopping, even if it has nothing to do with your story.

55

Do not miss the opportunity to warm up your third-person point of view.

Third-person point of view (POV) means everything is filtered through a character's head. The author keeps all thoughts and perceptions inside that character. In a "close" third-person novel, only one character is given this narrative platform. In "open" third-person, more than one character can be utilized—though it's best to limit POV to one character per scene (the "viewpoint character.")

Do not waste your third-person POV by making it sound like you, the author. Get deep into the head of the viewpoint character. Notice the difference between these two renditions:

Cool, Detached

Charlotte lifted her eyes, and in the mirror she could see two boys. Neither looked more than fifteen or sixteen. They may even have seemed like mere children trying to appear older. Each held a can of beer, even though it was against the rules. Both were bare from the waist up. One wore a towel around his waist, and flip-flops. He had soft skin. The other wore khaki shorts and boots. He was lean, with a large nose. He put his beer to his lips. Leaned his head back, and took a long drink. When he was finished, he doubled over, trembled, and said loudly, "It tastes so good when it hits your lips!"

Warm, Inside

Charlotte lifted her eyes, and in the mirror she could see two boys—mere boys! Neither looked more than fifteen or sixteen! Babies dropping their voices a couple of octaves in a desperate desire to sound like men! Each had a can of beer in his hand. *But this was not allowed!* Both were bare from the waist up. One wore a towel around his waist, only that and flip-flops. He had such a tender coating of baby fat over his cheeks, neck, and torso, it made Charlotte think of diapers and talcum powder. The other wore khaki shorts and boots. He was the leaner of the two but still at that mooncalf stage in which the nose looks enormous because the chin hasn't caught up with it yet. He threw his head back, lifted the can to his mouth, tilted it almost straight up, drank for what seemed like forever with his Adam's apple pumping up and down like a piston, then jackknifed his body and shook all over, as if in ecstasy, and cried out, "IT TASTES SO GOOD WHEN IT HITS YOUR LIPS!"

—*I Am Charlotte Simmons* by Tom Wolfe

In the second version, Wolfe uses heightened language, exclamation points and even capitals (a mark of his particular style) to render what the scene looks like to a naïve freshman in a coed dorm bathroom for the first time.

Another way to warm up your third-person POV is to make sure you find ways to filter all stimuli through the character.

For example, a student of mine opened her novel like this:

> Borden Glover held in his clutch and shifted his unibike into fourth gear. He wove through traffic on the new coast highway. The ocean surged along the bank.

Now, we know we are in Borden's head. Yet that last line is rather cool. It works, but can we warm it up?

> Borden Glover held in his clutch and shifted his unibike into fourth gear. He wove through traffic on the new coast highway, watching the ocean surge along the bank.

This small change warms up the POV. You can even give it more heat:

> He wove through traffic on the new coast highway, loving the sound and surge of the ocean along the bank.

Do these small changes make any real difference to the reader?

Yes, in ways they don't even realize. The accumulation of these small changes adds up to a much stronger reading experience.

That's really what all these tips and techniques are about, accumulating those little beats that, when added together, give a full and satisfying effect.

56

First-person point of view is the most intimate, thus requiring special handling.

Some people feel first-person POV is constraining because it doesn't let you jump to another scene in a different POV, or allow you to get into another character's head. Such constraints are also the strength of first–person POV, which gives the reader the most intimate view of a character.

There are several moves you can make within first person that work just as well as shifting from one point of view to another.

EMPLOY A TIME DELAY

I learned this from reading Phyllis Whitney, who did most of her suspense novels in first person. She'd sometimes end at a tense moment, then cut to the next scene, where the narrator is ahead in time, in a completely different setting or situation. But what happened back at the tense moment? Whitney strings you along until the narrator finally decides to recall it.

USE MULTIPLE FIRST-PERSON POV

Primarily a device used in literary fiction, the multiple first person gives you the opportunity to create intimacy with several characters. Some authors put the character name as a chapter title, to clue readers in on the switch.

As long as each voice is distinct and can carry its own weight, you can open up a story this way. This is an advanced technique, so I recommend you cut your teeth on pure first-person and third-person POV before you consider it.

VISIT ANOTHER HEAD

I know this sounds like *Being John Malkovich* or something, and in a way it is. The narrator can *speculate* about what is going on in the mind of another character.

For example, maybe you have a criminal on the run with a former girlfriend named Sarah. He might pause and think:

> I knew what Sarah would be thinking right about now, the sun going down, the lights of the city coming up. Yeah, she'd be thinking about it all right, the next guy to stab in the back. She'd be looking out her window, watching the business types getting out of cabs and stepping into the hotel for high-level meetings. Looking at them like items on a buffet table. *Who will it be next? Mmm, let's see, maybe I'll try an executive from San Francisco this time. Hmm …*

REVEAL INFORMATION
THROUGH ANOTHER CHARACTER

Your narrator can describe a scene as if in third person and reveal that he got the info from another character who was there. Lawrence Block opens *The Devil Knows You're Dead*:

> On the last Thursday in September, Lisa Holtzmann went shopping on Ninth Avenue. She got back to her apartment between three-thirty and four and made coffee. While it dripped through she replaced a burnt-out light bulb with one she'd just bought, put away her groceries, and read the recipe on the back of a box of Goya lentils. She was sitting at the window with a cup of coffee when the phone rang.
>
> It was Glenn, her husband, calling to tell her he wouldn't be home until around six-thirty.

The third-person style goes on for a few more paragraphs, until the narrator, Matt Scudder, says:

> I picture him sitting at the table in his shirt-sleeves—a blue pinpoint Oxford shirt, a button-down collar—and tossing his tie over one shoulder, to protect it from food stains. I'd seen him do that once, at a coffee shop called the Morning Star.

So how did Scudder know what to report about events he did not witness? He's an investigator for hire, so we come to understand he gathered the facts later. He also speculates about an action—tossing the tie—he had once observed. So what if it didn't happen in the "real" past? This is fiction, and Block uses the detail to set a mood.

You can also have another character report the facts of a scene to the narrator, then have the narrator render them as if in third person:

> "He starts leading me," Trip said, "and I thought about getting out of there, but something kept me going."
>
> "Your morbid curiosity?" I said.
>
> "Maybe saving your skin," he answered. "Why I do these things for you I don't know."
>
> "So what did you find?"
>
> Trip told me Morris had led him to a dilapidated guest house on the back property of a shabby house in the less desirable section of town. The railroad tracks were literally across the street. Scrub brush sprouted from every crack in the sidewalk, and the eucalyptus trees lining the street were in various stages of decay.
>
> Morris's place was a one-room, windowless shack that might have originally been designed to store tools. Now it was lined, floor to ceiling, with the detritus of a lifetime.
>
> Old man Morris was a classic pack-rat. Books, newspapers, vinyl record albums, shoes—including

two pairs of red and white bowling shoes, Trip noted—closed the quarters into a bizarre theater-in-the-round, with a small living space in the middle. A solitary mattress with an old Army blanket was the only piece of furniture, if one could call it that. The air inside was stale and heavy. [The scene can continue in this fashion, then cut back to the conversation the narrator is having with Trip in "real time."]

"Wow," I said when Trip was finished. "You meet the most interesting people."

COMBINE FIRST PERSON WITH THIRD PERSON

This is done quite a bit these days, especially in commercial fiction. Purists may rebel, arguing there is a jolt when you switch POV styles. But readers won't mind if you write compellingly in the different views. By that I mean that first-person narration should have its own unique attitude, distinguishable from the third-person POV by more than just using the pronoun *I*.

USE THE "IF I'D ONLY KNOWN ..." MOVE

Here's one move you can't do in third person, but only in first: The "if I'd only known" move. (This also can't be done in first-person present-tense style.) Because the first-person narrator is looking back in time, he can comment on what is *about* to happen, as well as what he's describing "onscreen." This is not to be done often, or too clunkily. Stephen King does it in *Christine*:

Then, near the end of that summer vacation, Arnie saw Christine for the first time and fell in love with her. I was with him that day—we were on our way home from work—and I would testify on the matter before the Throne of the Almighty God if called upon to do so.

Brother, he fell and he fell hard. It could have been funny if it hadn't been so sad, and if it hadn't gotten scary as quick as it did. It could have been funny if it hadn't been so bad. How bad was it?

It was bad from the start. And it got worse in a hurry.

The proper handling of point of view is one of the marks of a real pro. Study it often.

part III
STRATEGY

He whose ranks are united in purpose will be victorious.

—Sun Tzu

Fiction writers are strange beasts. They are, like all writers, observers first and foremost. Everything that happens to and around them is potential material for a story, and they look at it that way.

—Terry Brooks, *Sometimes the Magic Works: Lessons From a Writing Life*

You are a business, and your books are the product.

If you want to make it in the writing game, you must see yourself as others (namely, publishers) need to see you.

They need to see you as *valuable*. That's the foundation of any enterprise where money changes hands.

You will be published, and compensated, to the degree a publisher sees you bringing value to their table.

Pretty simple calculation.

But most writers don't like to think in these terms, especially if they are disposed to consider anything they write as sacred fire from the divine muse.

And we all know that from the writer's perspective, calling what we do a "business" is a little like calling the racetrack an "investment."

As thriller writer Joe Moore puts it, "How many normal people do you know who would work eighty to one hundred hours a week, seven days a week, with no benefits for two paychecks a year, and not know the amount of the checks until the publisher decides to send a statement?"

True that.

But to *increase your odds of success* you need to develop a little bit of the dispassion of the business executive.

First up, you need to do some *strategic planning* and *goal setting*.

I know this makes many of you shudder. Relax. The concepts are not that difficult, and they will help you in your goal to get published. Here we go.

STRATEGIC PLANNING FOR WRITERS

Start by thinking of yourself as a small business enterprise with you as your own board of directors. Now, sit down to plan and gaze into the future. You have only a finite time on this earth, so this exercise is to help you maximize your productivity and increase your quality.

That's what business is really all about.

Step 1: Cast Your Vision

Most successful businesses begin with some type of vision statement. This is the long-term, all-encompassing "dream" statement, describing what you want your career to look like.

Give yourself at least a day to begin drafting your vision. Go somewhere where you can be alone and just think about what you want to accomplish as a writer.

Begin at the end. Pretend you are looking back at your career ten years from now. What would you have it look like? What are some of the details? Don't worry about being "realistic" (whatever that means). Dream big and dream in detail.

Render the dream in a one-paragraph vision statement. Write this paragraph as if it has been accomplished.

Not:

> I hope to be a multi-published author of gripping mysteries ...

This way:

> I am a multi-published author of gripping mysteries ...

Include in your vision statement what you offer the market that distinguishes your writing from everyone else. Part of this includes your own *artistic vision*, what you want your writing to say.

> My mysteries not only have a style that moves to the rhythm of my city, in great sensory detail, but also comment on the resiliency of the human spirit.

Show your vision statement to someone you trust, and who knows you well. Get feedback. Rewrite it until it moves you.

You should, of course, revisit your vision statement periodically. Once a year is good. Go over it again and see if you need to make any changes.

Step 2: Count the Cost

The market is set up to reward excellence. Although it is imperfect in this regard, you must become excellent to have a shot. You must constantly strive to be *better*.

That means never "resting on your laurels."

It means a program of constant improvement. (See the section on "The career novelist will develop a writing improvement program, beginning with a notebook." on page 39.)

It means you have to count the cost. There are things you are going to have to do, and not do, in order to be a published writer. You will have to give up time in other pursuits. It's a good idea to talk this all over with your family and friends.

Do listen to them. But do not let them label you as crazy. Do not let them kill your dream. Make them partners instead.

> Work with all your intelligence and love. Work freely and rollickingly as though you were talking to a friend who loves you. Mentally (at least three or four times a day) thumb your nose at all know-it-alls, jeerers, critics, doubters.
>
> —Brenda Ueland, *If You Want to Write*

Step 3: Identify Your Critical Success Factors

Every enterprise has certain key factors that must be excellent in order for it to succeed. There are also factors for every person who works in a business. Writers have them, too. The critical factors are found within the following categories:

CRITICAL SUCCESS FACTORS

Start with the book. Your novel. You have nothing if you have no book.

There are two directions you have to go with the book. The first is to be the best writer you can be, which is a matter of working at your craft.

The second direction is bringing your book to the market, partnering with your publisher. That means you show a willingness to cooperate in the selling of your book, in whatever way you can *that does not harm your writing*. See "Promote as you will, but never let it affect your ability to write your best book." on page 243.

Now you must identify the critical success factors for learning your craft and for partnering with your publisher.

And you must decide to get better at them.

How do you do that? Set goals. That's the next step.

A goal is just a dream
unless it has legs.

There is a well-defined process for setting goals and realizing them. It goes like this:

1. DECIDE EXACTLY WHAT YOUR GOALS ARE.

Start with yearly goals. Maybe it's to finish one novel. Or two. Or one novel and two proposals. Whatever it is, make sure it's something you can measure.

It's very important to prioritize your goals via the ROE analysis.

ROE stands for "Return on Energy." You must determine what you truly want to accomplish and measure it by the expectation of return *and* the amount of energy you need to put into the enterprise.

Here's an illustration.

I love short stories. I love reading them and writing them. At the beginning of my writing career, I had to decide how much effort to put into short stories and novels.

Objectively speaking, the market for short stories is limited, and the financial returns minimal. Also, the short story, from my perspective, is the most difficult form of fiction. They require a ton of effort.

So I decided to concentrate on the novel, as the expected financial return is greater (and I wanted to make a living writing fiction). I did write a couple of short stories along the way, and got them published, but that was a sideline effort. For others, writing short stories may be what they want to do most, and the ROE is satisfaction and publication in a literary journal.

Here's another calculation. I love reading strange, experimental novels. I've even had some ideas along those lines. But experimental novels sell five copies. I want to be read. Does that mean I'll never take a flier on something out of the ordinary? No. But I wanted to keep the "main thing the main thing," and wrote commercial fiction, which I also love (if you don't love, in some way, what you're writing, write something else).

2. WRITE GOALS DOWN ON PAPER.

Why? Because you activate brainpower by doing this. The "boys in the basement" work even when you sleep. They like being given directions.

Read over your goals often. Daily is good. Re-prioritize as you see fit. But make sure you put something before your eyes.

Be as specific as possible, as in *I will* ...

> I will write 5,000 words a week.

> I will complete my novel by March 1.

I will find six agents who deal with my genre. I will do this by September 15.

On December 10, I will query the top three agents on my priority list.

3. MAKE PLANS.

Brainstorm *all* the things you have to do to reach your goals. You should also include all the obstacles to reaching your goals, and make plans either to remove the obstacles or work around them. If you cannot, then revise your goals to reflect your reality.

Prioritize the steps in your plan. Follow the 80/20 Rule (also know as the Pareto Principle). This means, in general, that 80 percent of your achievements come from 20 percent of your activities. That 20 percent makes up your "highest value activities."

For example, where is the best place for you to write? Is it in solitude and silence? Starbucks? A park bench? What time is best for you to write? Morning? Evening? Two A.M.? Make a list of these things and do more of them, not less.

4. TAKE SOME ACTION TOWARD YOUR GOALS IMMEDIATELY.

As soon as you've done steps 1 through 3, do something, however small, toward the realization of your goals. This may be as simple as writing one scene in your novel, jotting notes about your plot, or starting a voice journal for your Lead character.

Taking action immediately gives you a sense of momentum.

5. DO SOMETHING EVERY DAY TOWARD YOUR GOALS.

Refuse to be stopped. Keep up the daily momentum. Yes, you'll have some days that get away from you. That's normal. Don't beat yourself up. Your weekly quota can still be met. If a week doesn't go well, forget it and move on.

Just do something, each day, six days a week (see "Take a writing Sabbath and recharge your batteries." on page 199).

6. DECIDE, IN ADVANCE, YOU WILL NEVER QUIT.

You are a writer. Not someone who wants to write a novel. A *writer*.

> A writer who is a real writer is a rebel who never stops.
>
> —William Saroyan

7. REVIEW YOUR VISION AND GOALS EACH YEAR.

If you need to make revisions, make them. But keep the forward motion. Keep up the commitment to excellence.

8. ACT PROFESSIONALLY.

When you interact with others in the business, be professional about it. Remember:

- A professional is someone who does not waste someone else's time.

- A professional knows how to get to the point, knows what the other party is looking for.

- A professional produces, on time, what someone asks for, and presents it in the proper format.

9. CELEBRATE.

Find ways to give yourself a reward when you reach a goal. It's important to your morale, and you will need all the morale you can get if you want to get, and stay, published.

> You have to keep punching, because you've always got that puncher's chance.
>
> —Otis Chandler, publisher,
> *Los Angeles Times*

59

Network according to the law of reciprocity.

Your professional contacts are like spies who are on your side: Full of useful information and willing to help at the right time. This is networking.

But most people go about it all wrong. They see a potential contact solely as a means to an end. That makes them a taker, not a giver, and no one likes to associate with a taker.

Instead, you need to look at networking as *reciprocal*. The value of a contact is proportional to the value you bring to them.

> Be subtle! Be subtle! And use your spies for every kind of business.
>
> —Sun Tzu

That's why you should never join an online group just to hawk your work. Bring something *to* the group. Earn the right to talk about yourself and, when the opportunity comes up naturally, you'll be ready.

Here is a networking checklist:

1. Join groups and attend meetings.

2. Be a good listener. Utilize the 2-1 Rule: Try, by pointed questions, to get to know essential information about someone in two minutes. Give them, in return, your own essential information in one minute. Make your answer "low-key dazzling." That means you don't oversell yourself, but you don't sell yourself short, either.

3. Follow up any contacts with e-mails or short notes.

4. Keep a record of every contact, and the information you gleaned (e.g., family, kids, interests).

5. Prioritize contacts.

6. Don't be a gadfly. Only make occasional and appropriate contact.

7. If you run across an article online that might be of interest to a contact, send the link to them.

8. If something big happens (a contract, a great review, taking on an agent), let your contacts know. But don't tell them everything about your life.

9. In the words of Joseph Story, a former U.S. Supreme Court Justice, "Be brief, be pointed, let your matter stand lucid in order, solid and at hand; ..."

10. Review your contacts list frequently, expand it intentionally, and work it systematically.

60

Take a writing Sabbath and recharge your batteries.

Try to write six days a week, even if it's only one paragraph. The daily momentum is extremely important.

I realize some people have schedules that preclude this. (See "Become a snatcher of time, and maybe you'll hit 700 books, too." on page 200.)

But if you can write each day, do it, and meet a quota. Minimum 350 words a day. A baboon can do 350 words a day. Don't be shown up by a baboon.

Don't worry about making the words perfect. Just get them down. You can revise them later.

Then take a break, one day a week. I take one whole day off, and don't write a word. It recharges my batteries, freshens me up for the next day. I find I'm more creative and more energetic.

Taking a day off actually makes me more productive, not less. Amazing, but it works.

> He will win who knows when to fight and when not to fight.
>
> —Sun Tzu

61

Become a snatcher of time, and maybe you'll hit 700 books, too.

Isaac Asimov wrote more than 700 books. He had no other life, of course (he admitted as much), but that's still quite a haul.

How'd he do it?

One thing he copped to was snatching time to peck away at his typewriter. If he had a free fifteen minutes before dinner, rather than use that in casual conversation or watching the tube, or doing anything else for that matter, he saw it as an opportunity to get some writing in.

He had several typewriters around his apartment, each with a different project sitting in it. He'd pick one and type for fifteen minutes.

I like to snatch time. I've written a number of chapters on an AlphaSmart Neo, a nifty little dedicated word processor that fires up in one second and runs forever on AA batteries. For pure input of words, it's a lot more convenient than a laptop. It weighs about a pound. I hardly know I'm carrying it.

Use pads and pencils if you like, but find ways to snatch the occasional chunk of writing time. It all adds up.

Just remember not to snatch so much time you become a social pariah, an ingrate, or a hermit. "One may achieve remarkable writerly success while flunking all the major criteria for success as a human being," says Michael Bishop. "Try not to do that."

Try this exercise:

Print out a blank calendar of your typical week. Divide it up by the hour as illustrated in the sample on page 202.

Now, go through and darken every cell where you have a daily obligation, as illustrated on page 203. (You can do separate sheets for your weekends.)

You should see that there are many more blank cells than dark ones.

These represent potential "snatch writing" times. Plan for a few of these, just as you would an appointment.

Then be ready to take advantage of others that arise.

You will be amazed the rewards of this system.

> If, in the midst of difficulties, we are always ready
> to seize an advantage, we may extricate ourselves
> from misfortune.
>
> —Sun Tzu

WEEKLY TIME SHEET

	Sun	Mon	Tue	Wed	Thu	Fri	Sat
6:00							
7:00							
8:00							
9:00							
10:00							
11:00							
12:00							
1:00							
2:00							
3:00							
4:00							
5:00							
6:00							
7:00							
8:00							
9:00							
10:00							

	Mon	Tue	Wed	Thu	Fri
6:00					
7:00	■		■		■
8:00					
9:00	■	■	■	■	■
10:00	■	■	■	■	■
11:00					
12:00					
1:00					
2:00		■		■	
3:00					
4:00	■	■		■	■
5:00	■	■	■	■	■
6:00					
7:00	■	■			
8:00				■	
9:00				■	
10:00					

Know when to get an agent— and when not to.

Now consider the agent, usually the first priority of the aspiring writer with a manuscript in hand.

The search for an agent needs to be approached like any other battle in the long fight toward publication. It requires information, patience, and careful action.

Because a bad agent is worse than no agent.

That's right. Anyone can print up business cards and announce he is an "agent." Some of them will ask for various fees up front, or tell you to put your manuscript through an editing service that will take your money with no real guarantees.

Others will sign as many new writers as they can, then just send out their manuscripts to see if any stick. They do no nurturing of your career, and you can waste one, two, or maybe even more years with no real possibility of getting a contract.

With all this in mind, I asked literary agent Chip MacGregor of MacGregor Literary Agency for his pointers on when to get—and when not to get—an agent.

When Not to Get an Agent:

- When you're not a proven writer. Generally, publishers are looking for great ideas, expressed through great writing, and offered by a person with a great platform. Sometimes they get all three, but usually they settle for two of three. (I've taken on some unproven writers because I liked an idea or the writing, but understand that I work *much* harder for an unknown author, and get less return, than I do for a proven author ... and that's why agents prefer to work with proven authors.)

- When you don't have a full manuscript.

- When you won't let others critique your work.

- When you're not ready for rejection. This is a tough business. Do you have any idea how many times I hear the word "no" in a week? If you can't take "no," or if you can't take criticism, or if you can't take direction, go back to the dry-cleaning business. You obviously aren't tough enough for the writing biz.

- When you feel like you're "giving away" 15 percent of your income. I don't think any of the authors I work with resent my percentage ... they know I help them earn more than they'd get on their own. But if you don't feel that way, you're probably not ready to work with an agent.

- When you enjoy selling books and negotiating contracts, you have the relationships with editors to set up your own book deal, and you don't mind singing your own praises.

When to Get an Agent:

- When you have a dynamite proposal that a publisher will fall in love with. The agent should help you maximize the deal.

- When you don't know who to go to. An agent should have strong relationships in publishing ... *Always* ask a prospective agent who she represents, ask to talk with some of her authors, and ask what deals she has done lately. If an agent doesn't really represent anybody, or hasn't really done any deals, you have to wonder if she's really an agent or just playing one on TV. One more thought: An agent lives or dies on her relationships. Make sure you pick somebody who is good at relationships.

- When you don't know about contracts. They are legal documents that govern every aspect of your book for as long as it's in print ... a contract can impact your life for years.

- When you don't know what a good deal or a bad deal is.

- When you don't know how to read and understand a royalty statement.

- When you don't know how to market your book.

- When you don't have time on your hands and don't want to negotiate with the publisher yourself.

- When you don't want to be the person promoting or selling yourself and your work.

63

If you charge ahead without an agent, be sure you have something worth selling.

Yes, it's really hard to get published without an agent. But yes, it does happen. For it to happen to you, you will have to do the following:

1. Write a novel that will knock the socks off an editor. You will need feedback for this. You will need an excellent freelance editor (or two or three) and you'll have to have confirmation somehow that your novel meets the knocks-the-socks-off criterion. You are probably not the best judge of this.

2. Write a killer query letter and story synopsis (see "Your weapon for pursuing publication is the killer proposal." on page 219).

3. Find the right editors for your manuscript. You must absolutely be sure that the editor is interested in manuscripts of your type.

4. Have an irresistible pitch.

5. Get the pitch to the right editor via a query or face time. Face time happens at writers' conferences and events. If you can get yourself to a good writers' conference with that killer proposal and meet an editor and impress that editor, you may get an invitation to submit.

Sometimes lightning strikes and you get an offer.

So, should you look for an agent, then? You will need an experienced eye to help you go over your contract. Publishing contracts are ever more complex.

You can always hire a lawyer to do this. Not just any lawyer, by the way. Even if cousin Frank works for a big firm, that means nothing, because publishing contracts are a specialty.

If you have been in contact with an agent that you want to work with, share the happy news. If you already bring a deal to the table, agents are more inclined to want to work with you.

64

In the hunt for an agent,
take aim at more than one.

So how do you find an agent?

Have a famous author plead with their agent to take you on.

Or go to a writers' conference where you can meet agents face to face, and impress one or more with your pitch.

Or start the query process.

First, find out what agents are good. How? One way is to find out who represents successful authors in your genre. Look for acknowledgements in their books. Or get the information from author websites.

Get the latest edition of Writer's Digest Books' *Guide to Literary Agents* and wear it out.

Compile a list of at least two dozen agents who would be right for your kind of novel. Prioritize the list.

Visit the website of the agency and follow their submission guidelines. Check out an agent's track record. A reputable literary agent should have a website with a list of clients.

Avoid agents who charge reading fees or any other costs mandated before signing a representation agreement. Pass on any agency that has some sweetheart deal with an editing service or vanity press.

Simultaneously query the agents according to your prioritized list. How many at a time? Opinions vary, but half a dozen is a good rule of thumb. Why not the whole list? Because you first want a shot at your top prospects. You might get an offer from an agent near the bottom of your list, take it, then get a call from an agent at the top.

Agents know the biz, and they know writers looking for agents need go out simultaneously. If they don't know that, or announce they don't like it, pass on that agent. It is unfair and unbusinesslike to expect a writer to wait months at a time for a single query response before going out again.

Be sure your queries are personalized to the specific agent, mentioning why you have chosen them (e.g., you saw their listing in the *Guide to Literary Agents*).

This also applies to requests by agents to see a partial or full manuscript. It may be controversial to some that you would send actual material to more than one agent at a time, but you have only one life to live, and it's too short to wait months—sometimes up to a year!—for one response.

But what if an agent asks for an *exclusive* look at your partial or full? You will have to decide if you want to grant that, based upon your evaluation of the agent. A great agent is worth the wait, but not an open-ended wait.

What's a proper period of time for an exclusive look? That's not chiseled in stone, but four to six weeks seems long enough to evaluate a manuscript that's only sitting on one desk. Ask the agent what the policy is. Try to secure at least an informal time frame up front.

If you accept an offer of representation from an agent, notify any other agents who are considering your manuscript. Thank them for their time. That's good business practice.

Bottom line: Simultaneous submissions, of both queries and manuscripts, are understood by most agents to be the norm. It's business. It should be. Be polite and professional and you'll be respected in your efforts.

WHEN YOU DO GET AN AGENT ...

Be realistic. You have only one agent, but an agent has many clients. You cannot expect to be given all the attention. But if you continue to work at your craft and write books the agent can sell, getting attention won't be a problem.

65

Approach agents intelligently by knowing what they do and don't want.

Not long ago I sat in on a panel of ten literary agents. Here is the gist of what they said:

What Agents Want in an Author:

- Give me a fresh voice.

- Give me a one-line hook that makes me want to read more.

- The first couple of pages must draw me in.

- I want a client who is at least 95 percent "ready." I don't have the time to work with you if you're only 80 percent ready.

- Write what's in you.

On the Elusive Concept of "Voice":

- It's a combination of character, setting, and page turning.

- A distinctive style, like a Sergio Leone film.

- It's who you are.

- It's personality on the page.

- It's something written from your deepest truth.

- It is your expression as an artist.

Pet Peeves:

- Unrealistic comparisons to popular authors.

- When the synopsis doesn't tell me how the book ends.

- Sloppiness in presentation.

- Typos.

- Proposals sent to the wrong agent.

- Agent's name is misspelled.

- Not following an agent's submission guidelines.

- Omission of details: word count, genre, contact information including phone number.

- Cover letters that give your "life story."

- Obvious scattershot approach, rather than targeting the right agent.

- Opening pages that are mostly backstory, not actually a scene.

- Obvious first drafts.

On E-Mail Submissions:

- Treat it just like a printed submission. No fancy fonts and graphics.

- Make the cover letter a business letter, with contact information just as if on paper.

Unwise is the writer who quits his day job too soon.

In the back of virtually all fiction writers' minds lurks *the dream*: quitting the ol' day job and writing fiction full time.

Maybe the dream includes living in a cabin by a lake and writing all day as the birdies sing and the coffee brews. Or typing away in a tidy little condo in the city, while outside, on the street, harried commuters waste their lives driving to work.

Ah yes, the dream.

Is it all it's cracked up to be?

Let's think it through again. Consider:

1. Quitting your day job too soon may put negative pressure on your writing. You may be tempted to chase the market as your writing suffers. Remember, if you recognize a trend, it's usually too late to jump on the bandwagon.

2. The dream may not be anything close to realistic. It can get you high, but you come down real fast.

3. You need to have incredible desire and self-discipline to write full time. Novelist Stephanie

Grace Whitson says, "It takes determination, commitment, self-denial, self-control, and sometimes the ability to live on ramen noodles for days at a time."

> Oh, you hate your job? Why didn't you say so? There's a support group for that. It's called *everybody*, and they meet at the bar.
>
> —Drew Carey

4. You will need a financial plan. As a rule of thumb, you should have at least two books under contract and be receiving royalties (not just living off the dregs of your advance). Then you must determine how much per month you can live on, and make realistic adjustments.

5. Don't ignore the financial benefit of the day job. Author Sharon Dunn says, "A steady predictable paycheck contributes a great deal to peace of mind. Living in a constant state of panic every time a bill arrives makes focusing on various writing projects that much harder. Once you are an established writer, royalty payments still fluctuate."

6. A day job can keep you normal and connected to people. An agent was heard to remark that writers who quit their day jobs become "weird"

and demand more attention. There's something to that. Having a job where you interact with "normal" people can keep you grounded.

7. You can find plot and character ideas in your day job. As Stephen King notes in *On Writing*, people love to read about work. Even a mundane job can be an interesting background for a character if handled right.

Your weapon for pursuing publication is the killer proposal.

Every novelist needs to know how to put together a killer proposal.

The killer proposal is what gets your book to the next level of consideration, which is a request to see your full manuscript. It's what gets you through the first door.

The three pillars of the novel proposal are:

- the query letter
- the synopsis
- your first three chapters

A great query letter is like a firm handshake. It makes the recipient want to see what you're about. A bad letter is like a fish handshake or a *Hello* made with garlic breath.

A synopsis should read like jacket copy on steroids.

And then there are your first three chapters (some guidelines may ask for your first five or ten pages). Why the first three instead of just any three?

- Because if you send some middle chapters, the agent or editor will wonder what's wrong with your opening.

- The opening is what hooks readers. Editors and agents want to know you can do that.

By the way, the part of your proposal that usually read first is *page one of your sample chapters*. Why? Because it saves time. If you can't write, the reader doesn't have to bother with the rest of the package.

Good ROE for the reader.

What about a chapter-by-chapter outline? Submit that only if it is specifically requested. Otherwise, don't bother. There is no way to make an outline of chapters read well. Some novelists look at a book on proposal writing and mistakenly believe that the requirements of a fiction proposal are the same as a nonfiction book. Not so. Outlines are essential to the nonfiction proposal. They are fine in that context because they are giving hard information about the sections of the book.

But fiction is about story, and chapter outlines do not make for compelling narrative.

That's it. Letter, synopsis, sample chapters.

Now all you have to do is make each of them like Elizabeth Taylor in *A Place in the Sun*—irresistible. That is up to you and your material, of course. The concept and content of every story remains unique to the author.

But *how* you present you material in the proposal is key. If you'll keep it simple and follow the suggestions in the next few pages, presentation will never be a problem.

Your opening salvo is the killer query letter.

Abraham Lincoln was once asked how long a man's legs should be. He reportedly replied, "Long enough to reach the ground."

Lincoln could have written a great query letter.

Yours should be just long enough to get the basic information across with a *ka-ching* sound ringing softly in the background. Often, you will be submitting only the query letter at first (depending on the guidelines of a particular agent or editor), which is why *ka-ching* is all important. The reader needs to know: Does this book have a chance to sell copies? Is there a marketing hook here? How many people will actually be interested in this book once we spend the money to bring it out?

There's lots of advice floating around on how to write a query letter. Most of it says to begin with a short, introductory paragraph about what you're submitting and why (e.g., the agent represents this type of novel). If you do decide to start off that way, please do not do it like this writer, who submitted to an agent the following: "Dear Sir or Madam, Please bear with me, as I have a hard time putting my thoughts into words."

Of course, agents and editors see thousands upon thousands of versions of the same letter each year. Here is an alternative form that has the benefit of being a slight relief from the same old: Skip the introductory paragraph and get right to the plot. Why? Because that is what agents, editors, and readers are looking for in a writer: someone who can grab them from the start.

So grab.

This will make your basic letter three paragraphs long. (Of course, you *have* included your name, address, e-mail, and phone number at the top, as in a business letter. And you *have* addressed this letter to the correct person, and you know whether it's a Mr. or a Ms. And you have not used the person's full name, as in *Dear Joseph Agent*. That just looks strange. Follow this format even if you are submitting via e-mail.)

THE PLOT PARAGRAPH

Begin the plot paragraph with a one sentence logline (sometimes called a *tagline*). That's a catchy sentence that sums up the entire plot in a pleasing way. Such as:

> What if a shyster lawyer is magically forced to tell nothing but the truth for an entire day?

> A respected surgeon, wrongly convicted of murdering his wife, must elude capture by a team of U.S. Marshals until he finds the real killer.

> A lone New York cop is the only hope for dozens of hostages held by terrorists in a high rise building in LA.

Do you hear the *ka-ching*? You should. Unless you can generate a logline that has it, you're not ready to submit. Work and rework the line until it sings. Try it out on people. Excite total strangers with it. Would they be willing to give your book a try based on the logline alone?

Whether you write literary or commercial fiction, a potent logline is a must.

The rest of the plot paragraph is a story overview. Start your second sentence with the Lead character's name, occupation, and situation: *[Lead character] is a [occupation or vocation] who [life situation]*. This grounds the paragraph in "story reality." Then complete the paragraph as if it were a thirty-second movie trailer:

> Winter Massey is a former U.S. marshal who has made too many enemies on both sides of the law. Lucy Dockery is a judge's daughter who's never had to fight for anything in her life. But now Lucy and her young son have been kidnapped and sentenced to die—unless her father agrees to set a vicious criminal free. Massey is the closest thing to salvation they have, but he doesn't know that the beautiful FBI agent who brought him into the case may be playing a chilling double game—and that a

circle of treachery has begun to tighten around him. For Lucy, the time has come to scratch and claw for survival. For Massey, it's time to stop trusting the people he trusts most. Because in a storm of betrayal, there's only one way out.[1]

Train yourself to write the plot paragraph by reading the back cover copy of paperbacks and the editorial descriptions off Amazon.com.

THE BACKGROUND PARAGRAPH

Now give a paragraph with the title [don't italicize this, put it in CAPS as it is easier to read], genre, word count, and relevant parts of your background. Solid writing credits are good (more on that below). Experience in the field you're writing about is good. Where you were born and how much you love writing is not good. How well you think you'll do on TV interviews is horrible. Worst of all is saying your book is the "next" anything [James Patterson; Harry Potter] or is definitely going to be on the big screen as a major motion picture, and don't you, Mr. Agent or Ms. Editor, want to get in on that action?

Don't waste any time on how you came to write the story, what your grandmother and critique group think of it, or how the publisher should market you.

---

1 From John Ramsey Miller's novel *Side by Side*, adapted from his website. Used by permission.

If you had some interaction with the agent or editor at a conference, or heard her speak, or read something good on her blog, you can mention that. Briefly.

Legs just long enough to reach the ground:

> [TITLE] is a 95,000-word legal thriller. I've been a practicing lawyer for fourteen years. This is my first novel. I heard you speak at the Greater Downey Writers Conference and think this project will be a good fit for you.

The above is simple and gets the job done, which is to spur the reader to the sample chapters. If, however, your genre is somewhat creative (e.g., Amish-vampire), you should help the reader by placing it in context. If you can identify another successful novel, you can say that yours is "in the style of _____." If you're off the beaten track, you can sometimes come up with a combination of genres. *This novel is like 'Salem's Lot as if written by Beverly Lewis.*

Don't gild this lily, though, by intimating you are on that level or even better. Let the reader conclude that for herself as she reads your chapters.

What about publishing credits and training? Don't include nonfiction articles or poetry or anything else that doesn't show you know how to write a novel. Short stories in prestigious journals are good. Previous novels (if not too long ago) are also good. *Do not*, however, include a self-published novel as a "credit" (it's actually a debit).

If you have a degree in creative writing, say so. If you're a member of a quality organization (e.g., Mystery Writers of America; International Thriller Writers) you can include that. If you've taken a workshop from a well known teacher, yes.

If you have specialized knowledge (e.g., trial lawyer, FBI agent) that relates to the novel's subject matter, put that in.

Finally, if you have an endorsement *in hand* from a known writer, mention that. But don't say you plan to send your novel to Famous Writer and that you're confident he'll endorse it.

If, however, you can get Famous Writer to consent to read your manuscript, by all means pass along that bit of news.

THE THANK YOU PARAGRAPH

Thank you for your consideration.

Sincerely,

There is no need to add anything else here. No begging, pleading, or forced humor. This is a professional sign off, leaving the decision where it should be, in the reader's hands. The letter has done its job. Now it needs to get out of the way.

I'm not much for the concluding line, *I look forward to hearing from you.* Of course you do! That's why you spent all this time putting together a proposal. Just because you look forward to it doesn't get the reader all the more excited about responding.

The line won't hurt you, but it seems superfluous, and I like to avoid superfluity in all things professional.

BUT WHAT ABOUT MY "PLATFORM"?

The big buzzword in publishing these days is *platform.*

What is a platform? It's something you stand on. It comes from the world of speaking. You stand on a platform and yak at people, and if you're good at it, they pay you. And then you write a book and sell that at "the back of the room" and make more money. So does your publisher.

Platform has now been expanded to include any venue where you reach a significant audience, such as a popular blog. Platform will most often be applicable to nonfiction writers, those who have a subject that is of interest to a niche that can be identified and targeted.

Herein is the problem for fiction writers. We write for *readers of diverse interests,* so how do you find them?

Of course, if you *do* have a speaking platform related to an issue that pertains to your fiction, or have the following of a large list of devoted acolytes (note: most Twitter "followers" don't count as devoted), or a web presence of some magnitude (note: your mom and sister don't count as *magnitude*, but God love 'em for reading your blog), of course you should mention that. Put it in your background paragraph.

Do not include a dreamscape of all the things you *promise* to do to promote the book, such as appearing on *The Today Show* "should they ask." Such grandiosity is looked at with a jaundiced eye.

If, however, you can realistically help in the initial marketing phase—via speaking engagements, relationships with local bookstores, etc.—that can be included in the background paragraph.

Some writers have created complete, multiple-page marketing plans for their proposals, but it seems to me this smacks of overkill. Plus, these are very hard to do credibly unless you have a real background in business or marketing.

One agent told me she doesn't like query letters that "try too hard." A detailed marketing plan risks that feeling. The safer bet is to let your concept and content carry the load in establishing marketability.

ALL THE REST

And, of course, don't forget about these basic essentials:

1. No typos.

2. Single spaced, standard business letter format. I prefer block paragraphs (no indent) with a space between paragraphs. This is the easiest

form to read. You can use indents and no spaces between paragraphs if you prefer.

3. Don't send to the wrong person.

4. Don't misspell the right person's name.

5. Do not, ever, send an e-mail to multiple addresses simultaneously, so everyone can see everyone else's address. Rifle shot, not shotgun blast. Personalize every e-mail and letter.

6. Don't send the full manuscript until asked.

7. Don't be unprofessional, which means no fancy fonts (use Times or Times New Roman, or a traditional, easy to read serif font) or anything else that shouldn't be in a business letter.

8. Don't follow up a rejection with a letter of defense, scorn, bemusement, self-destructive urges or asking for a second chance based on something you've changed. Move on.

9. Keep it simple.

10. Follow all guidelines. For example, an agency might request that you send your query letter and the first x number of pages pasted right into the body of the e-mail. So you send only that much and no attachments. Give them what they ask for and no more.

69

Wow agents and editors by grabbing them with your opening chapters.

As stated above, the part of the proposal that is usually read first is page one of your sample chapters. Why? Because, if page one stinks, there is no reason to waste time on the rest (so the thinking goes). Thus, you've got to slay them from start. See "Speed is the essence of the opening," on page 119.

Remember:

1. The first line, or first paragraph at a minimum, must show a disturbance to the character's ordinary world.

2. Include dialogue on page one or two. Sharp dialogue is the fastest way, up front, to create confidence in the reader that you know what you're doing.

3. If your first chapter absolutely precludes the use of dialogue, consider throwing it out and making chapter two your new chapter one. You'll be amazed how often this improves your opening.

4. If you absolutely have to start without dialogue, make sure the scene *feels* like there could be dialogue, and get readers into a character's POV immediately.

5. Don't open with a long description of weather or setting, or with a dream.

6. End each chapter in a way that *forces* them to read on.

7. If your first three chapters don't add up to at least 3,000 words, add another chapter or two until you get there.

Remember that your opening chapters are *selling documents*. You're trying to sell a busy agent or editor on the idea of requesting your entire manuscript. They need to feel confident, immediately, that your story is one they can take to market.

Make the sale. Get the request for the full manuscript. Then, after you sign a book contract, you can take up the opening with your editor. But I'm going to bet by this time you'll love the one in your proposal, the one that helped you get published.

Utilize the principle of overcompensation to generate a killer synopsis.

A great novel synopsis is:

- compelling to read on its own
- all story (no introductions, interpretations, or author intrusion of any kind)
- written in present tense
- with capitalized character names the first time they're mentioned
- two to three pages, double spaced

I've called the killer synopsis *dust jacket copy on steroids*. Go to your bookshelf, bookstore, or library, and study a whole bunch of dust jackets from novels in your genre. Your synopsis should have a similar feel, but over two to three pages.

Remember, your synopsis is a tool to get the reader to request the whole manuscript. That's why it is only two to three pages. It "sells the sizzle, not the steak" as the ad folks used to say. It does its job and gets out of the way. And more and more agents and editors are asking for synopses of this length.

There used to be a rule of thumb of something like one page of synopsis for every 10,000 words of your novel. On the off chance you are asked to submit a synopsis of this length, *do one*. In fact, do one regardless. Do it no matter how painful it feels. Do it fast. Don't try to make it perfect. You are generating raw material.

Now, what do you do with those ten or more pages?

Boil them down into two to three pages of the good stuff. This is called overcompensation. Start big, then condense, and there's the synopsis you'll use.

The good news is, if you are asked for the longer one, then you've got one nearly ready. You now edit it the best you can. But at least you'll have the "first draft" of the longer synopsis already done.

Formatting:

- Use 1-inch margins all around.

- Double space your work.

- Single space your name, address, e-mail, and phone number in the upper left of the first page.

- One third of the way down, center the title in ALL CAPS and put Synopsis below that:

THE OLD MAN AND THE SEA
Synopsis

- Hit two returns, and start the synopsis. Use ragged right alignment for text:

> SANTIAGO, an old Cuban fisherman, has had a bad run of luck. Eighty-four days without a catch. The locals make fun of him. Because of this, his devoted young apprentice, MANOLIN, has been forced by his parents to leave Santiago for more promising fishermen. But each night, the boy sneaks back to help Santiago and talk about American baseball.
>
> Determined to get a catch the next day, Santiago sets out alone, deep into the waters of the Gulf Stream. He catches a tuna to use for bait. And then hooks a marlin. A big one. So big it drags his skiff so far out to sea Santiago can no longer see land. The fight is on.

- On page two, and all subsequent pages, put the following as a header, on the left and right sides, respectively:

Hemingway/THE OLD MAN AND THE SEA   Synopsis/(page #)

And that's all there is to formatting the synopsis. Keep it simple, so there is nothing to distract the reviewer from the story itself.

71

Always be ready to talk to someone in the elevator.

It's all the rage to talk about your "elevator speech." That's where you have thirty seconds to pitch your book, as if riding to the tenth floor with Steven Spielberg.

Or sitting across from an agent at a conference where you get to "speed date" for possible representation.

So just what is a good elevator speech?

You've already done it. *It's the opening paragraph of your query letter.*

Don't reinvent the wheel. That's not good ROE.

Just go over and over your query paragraph. When you give your elevator speech, deliver it with warmth and natural passion (don't hyperventilate). Don't stress about having it memorized word for word. You'll know enough of it to make it just fine.

Summarize your elevator pitch with a logline. That's a one-sentence summary that has as much *ka-ching* in it as possible. You can do this in two ways:

1. The "what if" line:

> What if a best-selling novelist becomes the incapacitated prisoner of his "number one fan"?

2. The "what happens" line:

> A middle-class gardener is given three days to come up with two million dollars to save his kidnapped wife.

Now you've got a logline and an elevator pitch in your back pocket. If someone asks you for a brief on your novel as you walk to the elevator (or anywhere else), you give the logline. If the person wants to know more, you give him the elevator speech.

Have a logline and an elevator speech for your current novel *and also* your novel in progress.

Don't have a novel in progress?

Start one.

> When I finish a novel, I ship the manuscript off to my editor, and while he's reading it, I begin a new one. I write half a dozen chapters and a brief synopsis—just enough to get my publishers hooked—then, as soon as I get the first check, I throw away the synopsis and let the book lead where it will. (My publishers have never complained about this.)
>
> —Stuart Woods

Plan your actions when attending a writers' conference, then work your plan.

A good writers' conference provides you opportunity for face time with fellow writers, sometimes readers, and industry professionals. This is not time to be squandered, especially since you're shelling out a lot of money to attend. Hearken to the following:

1. Plan ahead. Know who is going to be there. Make a prioritized list of who you'd like to meet and which speakers you'd like to hear.

2. Make appointments if you can. Sometimes you can sign up for these in advance. If you're polite and professional, you may be able to set them up at the conference. Do not expect to get every appointment you want. You can follow up with a polite e-mail afterward saying you're sorry you couldn't get together, mention the conference, and include a short pitch.

3. Always remember the two cardinal rules for the writers' conference attendee: Don't be dull and don't be desperate.

4. Talk to other attendees. Don't only focus on the celebrities or the industry people.

5. Don't come off as "me, me, me" all the time. Listen to other people. Ask *them* what they're writing. Let the conversation flow naturally after that.

6. Keep your tech at bay. Don't spend most of your time getting e-mail, texting, tweeting. Be with actual people in the actual moment.

7. Don't invite people into your social networking world right off the bat. Get to know them first. Remember, true networking is based on what *you* bring of value to the other person. See "Network according to the law of reciprocity," on page 197.

8. Jot notes on the back of business cards as soon as you can. Remember the key information you've gleaned from the contact. Mention it the first time you contact him.

9. Be a matchmaker. If you meet someone who might be interested in someone else you've met at the conference, get them together. Your estimated value to both of them will increase.

10. Treat everyone with respect, including the servers. Your vibe radiates outward.

73

"Never assume that a rejection of your stuff is also a rejection of you as a person ... unless it's accompanied by a punch in the nose."[1]

Writer Barnaby Conrad tells the story of a matador, all decked out in his "suit of lights," talking to a group of reporters outside the arena.

One reporter asks, "How did you happen to become a bullfighter?"

The matador replied, "I took up bullfighting because of the uncertainty of being a writer."

Truth be told, many of us would rather face the horns of an angry bull than another rejection letter. At least the bull isn't intimating that we can't write.

We also know rejection goes with the territory. No way to avoid it. But there *are* ways to keep rejection from becoming toxic, making you want to do a Sinatra: Roll yourself up in a big ball and dieeeee.

A rejection says one of two things: Either a piece isn't right for the publisher at that time, or it is not up to their

1 Quote from author Ron Goulart.

standards. The first is something you can't change; the second you can. You do it by learning to write better.

If, for some strange reason, someone were to tell you that you *personally* don't have what it takes to be a writer, you can be sure that someone is off his beam. How can anyone predict your future? Writing is a craft. People *can* learn how to write. No one has the capacity to tell you that you are the exception to the rule.

An obscure editor once told a future Nobel Prize winner: "I'm sorry, Mr. Kipling, but you just don't know how to use the English language." Kipling we remember. The editor no one can recall.

> I don't measure a man's success by how high he climbs but how high he bounces when he hits bottom.
>
> —General George S. Patton

It's also comforting to know that rejection happens to all writers, no matter how well known. Just remembering that fact helps enormously when a new rejection letter trembles in your fingers.

Such examples can also remind you of the value of persistence. One of my writing heroes, William Saroyan, collected a pile of rejection slips thirty inches high—some seven thousand—before he sold his first short story. Alex Haley, author of *Roots*, wrote every day, seven days a week, for *eight years* before selling to a small magazine. They stuck it out, and eventually broke through.

One of my favorite little books, *Rotten Rejections* from Pushcart Press, is a compendium of the setbacks some of our most famous writers received. For example:

Zane Grey, who became one of the best-selling authors in history, got this from an editor rejecting one of his early novels: "I do not see anything in this to convince me you can write either narrative or fiction."

Tony Hillerman sold millions of books about a Navajo police officer working on the reservation. An editor wrote him, "If you insist on rewriting this, get rid of all that Indian stuff."

Regarding *Animal Farm*, George Orwell was told, "It is impossible to sell animal stories in the U.S.A."

If it happened to them, it will happen to you. So always remember you're in good company. And keep writing!

The best rejection is constructive. Unfortunately, it is all too rare. Editors usually don't have the time or inclination to sit down and tell you where your manuscript may have gone wrong.

When one does take the time, though, treasure the advice. See what you can learn from it. And write a thank you note to the editor. It's not just the right thing to do; it will almost always be put in the "good graces" section of that editor's mind. This can be invaluable when you submit another piece to the same person.

When rejection comes with specificity, use it as a road sign. It will help you get closer to your eventual target—publication.

Just be sure to keep writing.

> Be done with the past, save where it serves to inspire you to greater and nobler effort. Be done with regrets over vanished opportunities, seeming failures, and bitter disappointments ... Be done with the "might have been," and think of the "shall be."
>
> —Grenville Kleiser

Promote as you will, but never let it affect your ability to write your best book.

The William Goldman axiom, *Nobody knows anything*, applies to promotion, too.

Which is why you should never allow yourself to obsess over it.

Here is my corollary to Goldman's Axiom: *Your success as a writer is inversely proportional to the anxiety you let yourself feel for promotion.*

Meaning, the more anxious you are about forcing success through self-promotional effort, the less creative energy you have for *the writing itself.*

Because the most important promotional tool you have is your best book.

Period.

Not Stephen King's best book, or Nora Roberts's. Yours. Heart, soul, skill, craft, passion, work, blood, tears, toil, and sweat. And even *then*, there's no guarantee. But at least you won't have diluted your strengths by obsessing over promotion.

Does that mean doing nothing? Sometimes. I know best-selling authors who do zip on self-promotion.

Here's a simple guideline: Do what you can without a) taking away from the quality of your writing time; b) taking away from the quality of personal relationships; and c) taking on debt.

So what are the ten best forms of self-promotion?

1. Your book.

2. Your book.

3. Your book.

4. Your web presence.

5. Reviews.

6. Publicity. Getting media attention is hard for the novelist, because the infotainment world is made up of nonfiction hooks. But if you can tie your novel to some issue of current interest, you have a chance of landing some interviews.

7. Face time. Bookstore signings, speaking gigs (start locally and work outward), and the like. Don't expect long lines. You're making readers "one at a time" as you can, and that takes time. But they're going to be quality readers if you have hit them with steps 1, 2, 3 and 8, 9, 10.

8. Your book.

9. Your book.

10. Your book.

SOCIAL NETWORKING MEDIA

A word about blogs, Facebook, Twitter, and whatever other social networking has come about since I wrote this:

Yes, do what you can, but always with ROE (Return on Energy) in mind. Some people believe there is a cumulative effect to these efforts. Maybe sometimes, and only if you give them massive amounts of time and quality. And even then, there is no guarantee of a large return. Not if your books don't deliver the goods.

And if your books *do* deliver the goods, word of mouth will do more than all your self-promotion efforts combined. Knowing that, you are free to invest as much time as you like in these things. Just remember, people aren't into reading glorified ads. You have to offer them something of value in everything you put out there. Such as useful information, entertainment, or provocation.

Do that, and you've earned the right to tell people all about yourself and your books from time to time.

> Half the money I spend on advertising is wasted; the trouble is, I don't know which half.
>
> —John Wanamaker,
> department store magnate

Nurture your relationship with a trusted ally, your editor.

Editors are people, too. So:

1. Be courteous. Editors get enough grief.

2. Be on time. Meeting deadlines will endear you to your editors, but they also understand that circumstances arise that may cause delays. The sooner you can anticipate these and tell your editor about them, the better.

3. Be open. I repeat: *Be open.* Editors want your book to be good, too.

4. Be firm if you want to insist on keeping something. But pick your fights judiciously. You can't go to the mat on everything.

5. Be grateful. Thank you notes, a nice gift basket on occasion—like Christmas or upon publication— these things are remembered.

For long-term success, design a typical writing day and stick to it.

Writing is, ultimately, a matter of cheeks on chair and words on page. You must develop a certain amount of discipline and as much of a schedule as you can.

Of course, all writers are not wired the same way. Some respond well to timetables and rigidity. Others need to hang loose. Know thyself, but go through the exercise of designing a schedule, and see if you can stick to it for a while. You can always tweak it later.

I've interviewed some of the best writers out there about their "typical" writing days. As you'll see, they are all across the board. Somewhere in the following is an idea or two you can adopt as your own.

> I start at 5:15 A.M. by flossing (always floss, every-one), then meditating (twenty minutes), then spend-ing forty-five minutes getting my kid (seventeen) up, breakfasted, and off to the bus for school. Then I clean the kitchen, make coffee, read the paper (fifteen minutes, mostly the sports), and finally take my second cup of joe up to my study where, by 8:30, I have answered a few e-mails and started writing.

The more I know what I am doing, the more time I can spend doing it. Five to six pages a day is my goal. After five hours, I often begin to get loopy. Then I begin taking breaks and answering more e-mails. By mid afternoon, I am asleep in my desk chair, hoping the phone will ring and wake me up.

—Michael Palmer

I don't know that I have ever been fortunate enough to have a typical writing day. If I ever do, it would go something like this: Get up, have coffee with my wife, answer e-mails, go to breakfast at one of our favorite places or eat it at home, then write until I run dry. Dinner with friends.

—Stephen Coonts

The word "typical" is not in my vocabulary. Right from the get-go, I was taught to think independently, to think outside the box, and, most importantly, to see the big picture. As I've already said, I'm thinking about a project 24/7. That means, for instance, I always have a pad and pen beside my bed. Invariably, in the midst of a novel, I'll have a fistful of thoughts the moment after I turn out the lights at night. I used to write only in the morning, but over the years, that's changed. Now I often don't get started writing until three or four in the afternoon. Why this is, I can't say;

writing is a basically irrational experience. And it's hard work, but try telling that to anyone who doesn't write.

—Eric Van Lustbader

When I'm under deadline it's nearly 24/7—well, maybe 18/7, and when I'm not, I actually go to the dentist, doctor, have the car washed, and go bowling. I always try to get in a little exercise and fun things with friends, but not when a deadline looms. If there's anything that's constant, it's that I'm a morning person and write in the mornings.

—Lisa Jackson

To be a productive writer you have to have an iron will. The Internet is probably the best and worst thing to ever happen to writers. It's great for research, but can be a terrible distraction when you need to focus on getting your work done. I have a goal of 2,500 words per day, which is about five single-spaced pages. As soon as the quota is hit, I get to go do something else, but during a typical day, I am normally at my desk the entire time. One of the tricks I learned from one of my writing professors at USC, Stanley Ralph Ross, was to never end the day at the end of a chapter. If that's where I am, I begin the next chapter and try to get a couple of sentences into it. This way

I'm not worried about where I should go next, I am already there. When I arrive at my desk the next day, the wheels are already spinning, and I'm excited about where my thriller is going.

—Brad Thor

I write five or six days a week. I make a huge effort to not work all seven days—which is all too easy for me to do. I spend one hour thinking about the book in the morning—walking or swimming—planning what I am going to write that day, where the book is going. Then I write from four to five hours writing during the first-draft process. From 12 P.M. to 2 P.M. and then 3 P.M. to 6 P.M. Give or take. In between, I take a walk, go get coffee, or talk on the phone. After the first draft (and I usually have three to four drafts), I usually work more than that—from six to nine hours.

—M.J. Rose

These days, I am no longer capable of the ten-hour stretches I used to put in, day after day, night after night. My workday begins around 11 in the morning, and there is a break for lunch around 1:30 or 1:45. At 2:00, while eating lunch, I wander through Llanview, Pennsylvania, an amazing little city where anything can happen: amnesia, resurrections, dopplegängers, serial killers, arson, rapes, visitations from the heavenly realms ... I'm telling you, in Llanview they live life with a capital L. At 3:30 or thereabouts, I return to my desk and work till about 7:00. If I get in five hours of work, it's a good day, and I know I've had it until the next time.

—Peter Straub

I find there's a ratio between thinking and writing, and when I'm just getting started on a book, the ratio is skewed heavily toward thinking, but as the story progresses and I figure things out, I can write more and need to think less. By the time I've reached the last 10 percent of the book, I've discovered the whole story out and it's pure writing—an electrifying feeling, like I've grabbed the back of a comet and am struggling just to hang on. So at the start of things, I spend a lot of time walking and thinking, and a 500-word day feels great. In the middle, I feel comfortable with 1,000 or so, and I'm spending more time in front of the computer. Two thousand always feels good. By the last third of the book, my average gets closer to 3,000, and I'm spending close to eight hours a day writing, with sanity breaks mixed in here and there. The most I've ever written in a day (twenty-two straight hours), with my fingers a blur and my hair on fire, was 8,200—the last two of which, not coincidentally, were "The End."

—Barry Eisler

There is no typical. In Florida, I write on the deck or in my office or by the kitchen counter. In Omaha it's on the screened-in porch or in the writing shed or late at night sitting up in bed. Sometimes I use a stand-up desk because I tend to pace. I write bits and pieces of chapters and dialogue in a notebook. Another notebook has all my research notes. These days, I force myself to use a laptop as much as possible because it's quicker, though I swear I think better in longhand. I still do what I like to call my writing marathons. I try to clear my schedule of appointments, distractions, engagements for at least a week at a time, and I write from morning until evening. I'm not a coffee drinker, but I've been known to guzzle pots of the stuff during my marathons. That's about as typical as I get.

—Alex Kava

77

To survive over any length of time, you must turn any criticism into a strength.

If you write for any length of time, you're going to get slammed by a critic. Doesn't even have to be a professional critic. It can be somebody in your writing group, or some anonymous Internet gadfly. Or your crazy uncle Phil.

Mickey Spillane was always being attacked by critics. In an interview, he said, "I don't pay any attention to them. Those guys, they get free books and then they try to tear you down. Critics themselves, they used to tear me up. ... At one point, I was the fifth most translated writer in world. Ahead of me were Lenin, Gorky, Tolstoy, and Jules Verne. It doesn't mean anything, but it's a funny thing to bring up. One day ... I'm at a tea party, if you can picture me at a tea party, and this guy comes up to me and says 'What a horrible commentary on the reading habits on Americans to think that you have seven of the top ten bestsellers of all time,' and I looked at him and I said, 'You're lucky I don't write three more books.'"

Spillane's wry dismissal is instructive. There are some critics who simply tear at you, and you can and should ignore them. There are others, however, who just might have a point to make that you can learn from.

So learn, glean, and ignore the rest. Treat it as a pain, a symptom that you show the doctor. He treats you, tells you how to get better, and sends you on your way.

> Every hour you spend writing is an hour not spent fretting about your writing.
>
> —Dennis Palumbo

When You Get Criticized:

1. Take a deep breath and don't do or think or say anything about it for a day. You'll feel it, of course. If you have to punch a pillow or eat an entire Bundt cake, go ahead.

2. The next day, consider the criticism with cool distance. Ask the following questions:

   a. Is there anything in here I immediately agree with? Be honest with yourself. Without honesty, you will miss opportunities for growth.

   b. Is there anything in here that is personal, rather than professional, criticism? Remember, if it's personal ("Dear, it's quite brave of you to continue to try to write, but at some point you must come to terms with the simple fact that you have no talent for this sort of thing") forget it. The critic is a dunce.

c. Once you have identified weak points in your writing, define them with specificity. For example, you may find that you are having trouble creating three-dimensional characters. Or your dialogue is flat. Whatever. Write down the challenge—and that's all it is, a challenge. Which is good. It forces you to get better.

d. Create a self-study program for tackling the problem area. See "The career novelist will develop a writing improvement program ..." on page 39.

WHAT TO DO WHEN IT REALLY HURTS

Let it hurt for half an hour, no more. Then get back to writing. Writing itself is the only known antidote for bad reviews, dings, nasty e-mails, returns, and skeptical relatives.

Then stand up from your next intense writing stint and shout, "I feel like a phoenix rising from Arizona!"[1]

1 Frank Costanza, *Seinfeld*.

A final word
from Sun Tzu, and me

> The commander stands for the virtues of wisdom,
> sincerity, benevolence, courage, and strictness.
>
> —Sun Tzu

If you want to take command of your writing life, attend
to Gen. Tzu in the following fashion:

WISDOM

The more you know about what you do, and the more
you do it, the wiser you will become *if you are open*. This
is not the place for you to have a chip on your shoulder.
The world of publishing does not care about the over-in-
flation of your self-estimation. Arrogance will not force
open the gates.

When you think about your career, be objective and
cool.

When you write, be as on fire as you can be.

It is wisdom to know when to use fire, and when to
use ice.

SINCERITY

The days of Sammy Glick are over. If you want to get anywhere, you have to be authentic. That not only means in your writing, but also in your dealings with other people.

Fred Allen, the old radio comedian, once said, "You can take all the sincerity in Hollywood and put it in a gnat's navel, and still have room for two caraway seeds and an agent's heart."

Make sure your sincerity is more expansive than that.

BENEVOLENCE

When Ryne Sandberg, the great Chicago Cubs second baseman, was inducted into the Baseball Hall of Fame, he said this in his speech:

"I was in awe every time I walked onto the field. That's respect. I was taught you never, ever disrespect your opponents or your teammates or your organization or your manager and never, ever your uniform. You make a great play, act like you've done it before; get a big hit, look for the third base coach and get ready to run the bases. ... Respect. A lot of people say this honor validates my career, but I didn't work hard for validation. I didn't play the game right because I saw a reward at the end of the tunnel. I played it right because that's what you're supposed to do, play it right and with respect. ... If this validates anything, it's that guys who taught me the game ... did what they were supposed to do, and I did what I was supposed to do."

Respect the craft of writing. Be in awe when you sit down at the keyboard or with a pen. Write hard, write with passion, because *that is what you do*. Don't waste any time dissing other writers or whining about how tough things are.

COURAGE

You know it takes courage to write.

It takes courage to write when you're not published and you don't have an agent.

It takes courage to write when you *are* published and you *do* have an agent. (This is why so many writers drink to excess, or anything else they can think of to drink to.)

You have it inside you to fight this fight. Write, think about what you write, then write some more.

Day by day. Year by year.

Do that, and you will jump ahead of 90 percent of the folks out there who want to get published.

Sun Tzu wrote: "The principle on which to manage an army is to set up one standard of courage which all must reach."

May you reach that standard in your own writing life.

May victory be yours.

STRICTNESS

You are responsible for your own self-discipline. No one can find the time for you, or write the words for you.

You must be strict with your standards, too. Don't settle for the easy, the familiar, the cliché.

And at the same time, do not let your aspirations and actions lead to anxiety and distress. Sun Tzu wrote: "To maintain discipline and calm ... this is the art of retaining self-control."

Onward.
Keep fighting.
Keep writing.

Index

About the Author

James Scott Bell is a best-selling novelist and popular writing teacher. His books for the Write Great Fiction series, *Plot & Structure* and *Revision & Self-Editing*, have become standards of the fiction craft. He lives in Los Angeles. His website is www.jamesscottbell.com